FISHERMAN
RESOURCES

BALM

HEALING FOR THE REPENTANT HEART

IN GILEAD

DUDLEY J. DELFFS

SHAW BOOKS

an imprint of WATERBROOK PRESS

Balm in Gilead
A SHAW BOOK
PUBLISHED BY WATERBROOK PRESS
2375 Telstar Drive, Suite 160
Colorado Springs, Colorado 80920
A division of Random House, Inc.

ISBN 0-87788-026-3

Published in association with the literary agency of Alive Communications, Inc., 7680 Goddard Street, Suite 200, Colorado Springs, CO 80920.

Printed in the United States of America
2002—First Edition

10 9 8 7 6 5 4 3 2 1

CONTENTS

A GOD OF HEALING

My heart is sore.

In my dream I toss it across an asphalt pavement, watching it skip like a stone. Just as I reach the spot where it lands, my heart lurches forward with the wind, beyond my grasp, battered against the boulders up ahead. This painful game of tag continues until I corner myself in a nest of fallen branches.

When I retrieve it, cradling it in my hands, my heart is pockmarked and scarred from bouncing along the hard surfaces. Raw and tender, it needs rest and healing, time to recover from the numerous scrapes along the trail. Somehow I can't place it back inside of me where it belongs until I've tended to its wounds. My heart is sore, and I'm out of breath from chasing it.

It doesn't take a Joseph to help me interpret my dream. For the past three years, I have been teaching full time, attending graduate school, and trying to complete a novel. I miss being fully present for my wife and three children in the ways that I long to be. My parents' struggles with illness and injury leave me hurting and afraid for them. Financial pressures often make each month a faith challenge. But throughout this frenetic season, I have become much more aware of the vital importance of stilling myself before my Father, of attending to the true needs of my battle-weary heart.

I'm guessing your heart is just as sore and weary as my own, if not more. Perhaps it took a vivid dream like mine, or the weight of another task or responsibility, or simply a quiet moment amid the daily rush to signal that your heart is hurting, to lead you to a breathless realization of who you've become or Who you've lost sight of.

And maybe, like me, you've tried to make time for yourself, tried to rest, tried to pray more, tried to force yourself to connect with God. We both know that the relief we crave is found only in relationship with him, the Triune God: Abba Father, the Savior Son, and the Spirit of Life. We've attempted to set aside a quiet time for reading his Word, for reflecting and praying, for listening. But the clamor of our life's pressures and the ravenous appetite of our schedules intrude and distract us. We lose our way again until we're swallowed by the wild current of events and emotions sweeping us away. Then our attempts become compounded by guilt and weariness until the next tide comes in.

How do we break this whirlpool cycle? How do we focus our efforts toward a rekindled passion for our Lord, not just another daily accomplishment or failure? The solution to our desire for rest and renewal is simple and life threatening: repentance. It means turning away from ourselves and moving toward God. This process in our Christian journey is probably not new—that's the simple part. But it is ongoing and deliberate, and that's the part that threatens the way we want to live our lives. Repentance is far more than reciting our sins before God. It is a deep transforming work of God's Spirit. It is the pathway to inward healing. Yet how many of us deliberately take time out for repentant self-reflection?

IS THERE NO BALM IN GILEAD?

When guilt, anxiety, or old wounds cause us to drift away from God—to chase after our own wind-blown hearts in a wearying pursuit for wholeness—repentance can realign our spiritual compass. It gives us an opportunity to step back from roles and responsibilities in order to reflect on how closely attuned we are to God's presence and work in our lives. Spiritual retreats often facilitate this "spring cleaning" of the soul, but most of us are rarely able to drop everything and get away.

Such a desire for cleansing refreshment is nothing new. In the ancient world, Gilead, a fertile region just west of the Jordan River, attracted thousands of visitors to its thick balsam groves. The oil distilled from the sap of the balsams soothed aching muscles, healed open wounds, and reinvigorated tired bodies. The oil's fragrance, so redolent of evergreen and river breezes, was heralded as an aphrodisiac. It's no coincidence, then, that the prophet Jeremiah chose this amazing balm as a metaphor for Israel's needs: "Is there no balm in Gilead? Is there no physician there? Why then is there no healing for the wound of my people?" (Jeremiah 8:22).

The Israelites would have recognized the irony in the prophet's questions: If any place afforded healing, it was the resortlike hills of Gilead, complete with balsam oils, herbal remedies, and assorted doctors. Yet the Jewish people were hurting and struggling because they had turned away from the inward balm of repentance and rest that God offered them.

We find ourselves in the same dilemma today, suffering from wounds God wants to heal. He invites us to turn our hearts back toward him, to draw close to our Abba's heart. As we personally awaken to Jeremiah's question, the lyrics of an old African American spiritual affirm God's offer: "There is a balm in Gilead to make the wounded whole; / There is a balm in Gilead to heal the sin-sick soul."

WOUNDS GOD WANTS TO HEAL

Balm in Gilead has been written to lead you into a deeper experience of God's life-changing love through a cleansing interlude of repentance. In eight sessions, you will be guided through exercises in Bible study, prayer, and self-reflection designed to help you direct your attention to what

God is doing in your life. Following these sessions you'll find a "Commencement" section that invites you to go on a spiritual retreat. You might want to take this retreat before you read the book as well as after you finish it.

As you respond to God's invitation to draw closer to him, you may want to use this devotional guide with a prayer partner or a small group. Or you may simply prefer to spend time alone basking in the presence of the One who loves you most. Wherever you are in your spiritual journey and whatever personal circumstances you face, you can receive more of God's grace. Not by trying harder, but by setting down the burdens you are carrying and experiencing renewal through the gifts of self-reflection, confession, grace, forgiveness, gratitude, obedience, suffering, and community.

Each session explores one of these gifts and its role in healing our repentant hearts by drawing us closer to the heart of our Abba Father. You'll notice that each chapter title conveys a medical-physical metaphor—for example, "Grace: An Aching Cure." This is an attempt to reflect both our dis-ease and the balm God provides for us. While you may move through each session in order, feel free to skip around and explore each one as you choose or feel led. There is no set order or progression other than moving from where you are toward a closer relationship with God. If you are going through the book in a group setting, you could choose to read each chapter between meetings, or you may want to read the chapters aloud during your times together.

Within each session you will find some opening thoughts from my own life, followed by a question or two (called "Breaking Ground") to help you relate to the material's focus. You'll then explore a relevant Scripture passage and begin observing what takes place by answering a series of questions called "First Looks." After reading some expository comments on the passage, you'll move into a series of questions called "Taking It In." Finally, in "Making It Real," you'll be invited to consider the implications and applications of the passage to your own needs and spiritual journey.

To reinforce the relevance of each chapter to the rest of your life, a "Spiritual Therapy" section will offer suggestions for hands-on ways to practice and experience the central point of each chapter. If you're going through this study with a partner or in a small group, you may want to do this "Spiritual Therapy" section between meetings and then talk at your next meeting about your experiences from the previous chapter before starting the next chapter. If you are completing this study on your own, you might want to keep a journal to record your thoughts, feelings, and reactions to what you're experiencing. A journal can be invaluable in helping you chart your spiritual growth, especially during a busy or hectic season of life.

To enhance the take-away value of this book, a multimedia bibliography is provided at the end of each chapter as a kind of spiritual medicine cabinet, enabling you to reflect in more personal, private ways. These bibliographies offer suggestions for books, movies, and music that you can experience individually or as a group. Not every book or movie listed may be appropriate or meaningful for every reader, so use discretion. If you're going through this study in a group, you might enjoy watching one of the films together—if everyone approves of the particular movie and its rating—before moving on to the next chapter, or you may want to listen to one of the suggested pieces of music before each group. These are only suggestions, but they may prompt you to think of more original ideas for your own personal integration and reflection.

Finally, at the end of the book, you'll find "Leader's Notes". Questions from the sessions that have leader's notes are marked with a ✐ in the text. If you are going through this study in a group, the leader's notes may help guide the group to reflective answers on some of the more involved questions. The notes can also be valuable if you are going through the book individually and need some prompting on a question.

The Journey of the Repentant Heart

Regardless of how you proceed, my prayer is that our Father will soothe and heal you with the balm of Gilead, the fragrant distillation of repentance. To start you on this process, I encourage you to think through the following questions. To pray about your honest responses. And perhaps even to write down some of your feelings and thoughts. Regardless of how you decide to proceed and use this study, identifying your own starting point can be invaluable in tracking your past journey, avoiding present pitfalls, and navigating your path ahead. Godspeed!

Questions to Consider Before You Begin

1. In what ways has God spoken to you about your own heart's soreness? What have you done in the past to try to find rest and relief?

2. What's your impression so far concerning the relationship between repentance and healing? In what ways do you think the two are related?

3. How are you hoping this study will facilitate your relationship with God? In what ways would you like it to help you?

4. What changes would you like to see in your life by the time you complete this study?

SELF-REFLECTION:
A SPIRITUAL CHECKUP

JOHN 5:2-14

Come to me, all you who are weary and burdened,
and I will give you rest. Take my yoke upon you and
learn from me, for I am gentle and humble in heart,
and you will find rest for your souls. For my yoke is
easy and my burden is light.

—MATTHEW 11:28-30

In William Faulkner's novel *As I Lay Dying,* the character Darl observes, "In a strange room you must empty yourself for sleep." Darl elaborates on the mystery of laying down his defenses and reminding himself who he really is before he can rest. I believe the process of repentance often begins the same way, especially if we want to experience fully the rest and heal-ing that God offers as we move closer to him. We must empty ourselves of the self-in-control, the defensive roles, and the attitudes that often char-acterize our lives. We must peel away the accumulated layers of self-involvement, selfishness, and idolatry that separate us from our Father's love. We must present ourselves before him with honesty.

BREAKING GROUND

How do you prepare for bed each night, especially in an unfamiliar place? How do you relate to Darl's observation about "emptying" yourself for sleep?

⌇∘⌇

Most pilots will tell you that it's hard to reach an intended destination if the navigator doesn't know the coordinates of the place from which the flight originates. Similarly, we must prayerfully and quietly consider our starting place in order to clarify where we are on the Christian journey and where we want to be. Spiritual renewal requires time for self-reflection and self-assessment. We identify our present location in order to assess the distance between us and God, to reset our heart's compass at true north in our desire for him.

Self-reflection, however, can easily hijack our souls and send us back to our starting point—ourselves. An attempt at honest reflection can become self-absorption, and our desire for relief and healing can begin to outweigh our love of God and our desire for his purposes. How do we avoid such a detour? How can we ask ourselves some hard questions about our relationship with God without making our feelings the focus?

In John's gospel we find a story of healing that offers clues about how to undertake a repentant self-examination. **Read John 5:2-14** and notice the way Jesus relates to the lame man in this encounter.

You may be asking yourself, *How does this story of physical healing relate to self-reflection and repentance?* A good question, but let's work through the following study questions before answering it.

FIRST LOOKS

1. What is the setting for this encounter? Why is it important

that we know a little about this place before we read about the
rest of the encounter?

2. What did Jesus first ask the lame man? Did the man respond
   to Jesus directly? Did he ask for healing?

3. What did the Jewish leaders ask the lame man after his
   healing?

4. Where did Jesus next encounter this man? What is the basis
   for their conversation?

What was the man's response to Jesus' final admonition?

The setting for this scene depicts a busy place of healing for physical ailments. Traditionally, the pool at Bethesda was a holy place where angels would stir the water, and those with ailments would be healed if they reached the moving water first. Ironically, the lame man spent immeasurable time beside the pool, where healing was within his sight but beyond his ability to grasp. The physical ailment for which he desired healing kept him from the wellness before him. His encounter with Jesus, whom we later learn the man does not recognize, is brief and dramatic. Nonetheless, it is densely packed with implications and interpretive opportunities. Let's consider some of them in the following questions.

Taking It In

5. Jesus asked the lame man if he wanted to get well (verse 6). Why would Jesus, knowing the man has been lame for most of his life, ask a question with such an "obvious" answer?

Does Jesus' approach surprise you? Why or why not?

6. According to verse 7, what did the lame man see as his greatest need? Notice that he did not ask Jesus for help but only described his situation. Why do you suppose he didn't ask directly for assistance into the pool? What did Jesus consider

to be this man's greatest need? Why do you think so? (See verses 6,8,14.)

7. Why do you think Jesus told the man to pick up his mat if it violated Sabbath law? What was Jesus' priority in this encounter with the lame man?

8. How do you interpret Jesus' final words to the healed man in the temple—a warning, an observation, friendly advice? What do you suppose the "something worse" might be if the healed man doesn't stop sinning?

What first strikes me about this scene is Jesus' question after learning of the lame man's situation: "Do you want to get well?" It might seem cruel if you or I were to ask a paraplegic in a doctor's office the same question.

But here we must trust the perfect loving nature of the Messiah. What might his motive be in using such an approach to this man and his affliction? It might have something to do with Jesus' understanding of human nature. While the lame man was clearly focused on his physical liability, Jesus was concerned about wholeness of spirit as well. He knew that the lame man could not be healed unless he was willing to move beyond what had clearly preoccupied him for the previous thirty-eight years.

Jesus sees us, like the lame man, longing for healing. He comes to where we are and asks our hearts, "Do you want to get well?" This is not a rhetorical question with an obvious answer, but a soul-challenging inquiry into our true desires. The implication seems to be that if we truly desire wellness, we must move beyond the apparent barriers that often limit our perception of how we relate to God (and others). We will likely have to leave the old hurts and wounds behind us—along with the conditions and excuses they often provide us—and obey the Savior's command.

We must also move beyond the qualifications we might tack on to Jesus' question: "Yes, I want to be well, as long as it doesn't hurt too much or cost too much or ask too much of me." But we must be willing to answer the question directly and honestly, without qualification or concern for our definition of wellness. The lame man does not respond to Jesus' question with fear, doubt, or bitterness. His suffering is such that he wants wellness regardless of what it might cost him. He is focused on getting into the pool, beating out the others who are there with him, and being healed of the present ailment that has plagued him for so long. He doesn't ask the intriguing Stranger directly for help, but he clearly implies his physical need for help getting into the pool. Perhaps the Stranger could offer a pair of strong arms to boost him into the water ahead of others? Whether the lame man is ignorant of his greater need for forgiveness of sins and for inner healing, or whether his physical ailment eclipses all other needs, we cannot tell. Nonetheless, the man acts when the Stranger speaks to his physical need.

Jesus dramatically commands the man to take up his mat and walk—he is instantly healed and has encountered the living Messiah face to face. The incredulous man goes on his way, the recipient of an incredible gift that he has not dared imagine outside of his own perceptions of how healing could occur in the pool.

But what about the rest of the story? And how does it correspond to our desire for honest self-reflection leading to repentance? The following questions will provide you with some starting points.

MAKING IT REAL

9. Put yourself in the lame man's place. Why have you continued to wait beside the pool all these years?

How have your hopes changed since you first came to Bethesda?

◈ 10. Name one area in your life right now where you are wounded or paralyzed. What would healing in that area look like?

◈ *Indicates further information in Leader's Notes*

How close have you placed yourself to the healing pool?
What are your current hopes for healing?

What are you waiting for so that healing can occur?

🖉 11.   What would it look like for you to "pick up your mat and
walk"? In other words, what steps do you need to take in order
to pursue intimacy with God and healing for yourself?

12. Do you want to be well? What is your answer to Jesus' question based on the way you're currently living your life?

13. Note how the Jewish leaders ignored the lame man's healing and focused on the breaking of the Sabbath law. They were less interested in wellness and more concerned about self-righteous rules. In what ways has legalism hindered your past efforts at healing and renewal? Is it easier for you to identify with the lame man or with the Jewish leaders? Why?

14. Does Jesus' encounter with the lame man remind you of an encounter that you have had with Christ? What emotions or thoughts come to mind when you think of that experience? How has God's faithfulness in the past brought you to this present point of desiring repentance and healing?

In the final exchange with the man from Bethesda, Jesus once again states the seemingly obvious: "See, you are well again" (verse 14). It is as if the man needs a reminder about the truth of his new condition, a reminder that he has gotten what he has wanted for most of his life. We might wonder whether the once-lame man fully understands the life-changing implications of his healing. While both he and the Jewish leaders can see that he is now able to walk, they do not readily embrace the reality of it. Perhaps they do not want to examine the implications because such exploration would intrude into their lives, requiring other choices—less self-centered, less manageable choices—about the way they relate to God and identify themselves.

But the healed man cannot deny the physical and personal transformation despite the efforts of the Pharisees to deny that Jesus is the Messiah. This leads us to Christ's final words to the man: "Stop sinning or something worse may happen to you" (verse 14). What is Jesus saying here? Surely he doesn't expect the man to be divine in nature just because his body is healed. This final admonition seems to parallel Jesus' opening question to the man, "Do you want to get well?" Both appeal to the man's volition, his ability to act based on deliberate choices.

While numerous readers and scholars disagree as to what the "something worse" consequence of a return to sinning might have been, I believe that Jesus wanted to distinguish between the man's future and his previous thirty-eight years of life. As with any of us, if this man had a dramatic encounter with the Messiah and then returned to sinning, he would face far worse eternal consequences than a temporary physical affliction.

SPIRITUAL THERAPY

As you reflect on the passage of Scripture in the study and its application to the "starting point" of your own soul, prayerfully consider what the barriers are to your own repentance and healing. Use the following list as a starting point, but I encourage you to add your own more specific items to the list.

Look over the following areas of struggle. While you're free to check all the areas that apply, you might prioritize two or three for the duration of this study and journal your responses to some of the parenthetical questions.

Areas that contribute to my own lameness of spirit:

_____ Fear (What are you afraid of? Be specific.)

_____ Anger (List the sources of your anger.)

_____ Jealousy (Of what or whom are you jealous? Why?)

_____ Old Wounds (What are they? How do they currently manifest themselves in your life?)

_____ Ongoing Struggles (What struggles are ongoing for you? How do you currently address them?)

_____ Guilt/Shame (In what ways have you responded to these feelings in the past? Now?)

_____ Busyness (How ready are you to refocus your priorities? Why?)

_____ Depression (What influences or contributes to your depression?)

_____ Grief (What and/or whom have you lost? How have you expressed your grief up to now?)

_____ Other (List your own additional struggles.)

Certainly each one of these areas is a large category of human experience unto itself. But consider the conflict and tension they exert in your present spiritual journey. Who would you be without these struggles? Why? What would your relationship with God be like if you experienced healing in these areas? Reflect on these questions in at least one designated prayer time this week. You might want to journal your feelings and ideas about these questions and this chapter. You might want to share your thoughts and feelings with a close friend or family member.

RESOURCE BIBLIOGRAPHY

Books

Dakota: A Spiritual Geography, Kathleen Norris, memoir—A New York
 poet returns to her Midwestern family roots and faith.

The Hours, Michael Cunningham, novel—Explores the lives of three
 women as they reflect on their internal motivations and their
 relationships with family and friends.

My Name Is Asher Lev, Chaim Potok, novel—An artist comes of age
 amidst his family's Jewish culture and religious limitations.

A River Runs Through It, Norman McLean, novella—A story set in
 rugged Montana that explores family dynamics and the various
 catalysts for change in how members love and relate to one
 another.

Traveling Mercies, Anne Lamott, autobiographical nonfiction—An honest and achingly funny memoir of a woman recovering her life
 while discovering her faith.

Films

Castaway—After surviving a plane crash on a desert island, a man confronts his loneliness and purpose in life before returning to the
 roles he left behind.

Joe vs. the Volcano—Joe faces the nature of suffering and questions what
 he has always valued most in life.

Phenomenon—A small-town man discovers amazing powers prior to his
 being diagnosed with a terminal disease.

Regarding Henry—A yuppie lawyer recovers from a head wound and
 rediscovers his priorities, his family, and his integrity.

Wit, stage play adaptation—A vivid meditation by a female English pro-
 fessor dying of cancer in which she reflects on God, the nature
 of suffering, and the legacy she will leave behind. (This con-

tains graphic scenes of the effects of chemotherapy as well as graphic language and may not be well suited for some viewers.)

Music

"Appalachian Spring," Aaron Copland—A perennial favorite of twentieth-century American orchestral music, reminding listeners of the joys of rebirth and renewal after desolate winters.

"Canon in D major," Johann Pachelbel—A lovely, meditative canon that unfolds classical beauty in simplicity and repetition.

"Quartet no. 15 in G," Franz Schubert—A great classical suite for meditation that reflects intensity, soothing harmonies, and beautiful melodies.

Confession:
Open-Heart Surgery

1 John 1:8–2:11

You do not delight in sacrifice, or I would bring it;
You do not take pleasure in burnt offerings.
The sacrifices of God are a broken spirit;
A broken and contrite heart,
O God, you will not despise.

—Psalm 51:16-17

The patient lies motionless, draped in surgical green in the center of the operating theater. Masked doctors and nurses move gloved hands through an assembly-line production of steel instruments and plastic tubes. The heart has been blocked in its efforts to pump blood throughout the patient's body. One artery looks like a straw that has been shellacked shut from the inside. Another allows only a tiny, threadlike stream of blood to pass. Without the operation, the flow will cease altogether, like a river evaporated by a summer's drought. Depleted blood will not be filtered, restored with oxygen, and circulated throughout the body. With a successful operation, however, the blocked paths will once again open to allow the heart mechanism to send its life stream coursing at regular intervals.

As melodramatic as it may seem, this portrait of renewed life occurs just as often in the church pew as it does in the emergency room. Just as an operation unclogs the cholesterol-induced plaque lining the heart's arteries, confession relieves the buildup of layers of self-interest around our hearts. The lifeblood of the Christian life, the gift of God's grace, can only circulate when we remove ourselves from the center of our lives by acknowledging our sins and embracing his forgiveness. While we may acknowledge our need for confession, the discipline of practicing it may be sorely lacking.

BREAKING GROUND

How have you practiced confession in the past? Alone or confessing to someone else? In conversational prayer or by using Scripture or a prescribed prayer? At regular intervals or whenever it happens to come to mind? Do you tend to confess a specific sin immediately after you recognize it, or do you often wait until you have a "grocery list"? What factors have shaped your view of confession and its role in your Christian journey?

∽o∾

In the Japanese language, a single word may require an entire sentence in English to express its meaning. Such is the case with the word *jiko-chushin*, which might be translated literally into English as "one who puts the self in the middle of the heart." Similarly, perhaps some of you recall an old parachurch evangelistic tract that depicted our lives as thrones and our need to remove ourselves from royal command and abdicate to Christ. Whether our commitment to follow Jesus was made years ago or just last week, we find that this process of prying ourselves off the throne of our lives, of breaking into our own *jiko-chushin*, is ongoing. Confession serves as the fulcrum for such an unnatural, yet supernatural, process.

And although the process of our renewal is supernatural, we still may ask: How is confession able to chisel away the self-lined trenches of our heart? How does it facilitate the ongoing process of our sanctification? And how does it afford us healing and spiritual rest, especially when it feels so laborious sometimes? While I believe these are questions more to be lived out than answered definitively, we can gain insight into them by examining the words of one of Christ's apostles. **Read 1 John 1:8–2:11.**

Since John seems to address the role of confession so straightforwardly in this passage, you might wonder how he delineates the process of cleansing that happens when we acknowledge our sins before God. I believe that if we examine the apostle's words carefully, they yield a glimpse of the Master Surgeon's scalpel.

First Looks

1. Whom did John address in this letter? Why was he writing to them (2:1)?

2. According to John, what happens "if we confess our sins" (1:9)? What happens if we don't confess? What words describe God's character in 1:8-10? What words or phrases describe us?

3. John used several contrasting pairs of words or images throughout this passage. See if you can identify three of these pairs.

4. According to John's explanation in 2:3-6, how do we know if we are in fellowship with God?

How did John repeat this idea throughout the passage?

5. How did John describe the relationship between what someone claims and what someone does (1:8-10)? What illustration or diagram did he use to depict this relationship between words and actions (2:3-6)? How did he describe the believer who claims to love but acts in hate (2:9-11)?

Most scholars agree that the first letter of the apostle John was written to a group of believers in the early church who were suddenly confronted with false teachers and philosophers after Christ's resurrection and ascension. John logically tries to make the basics clear regarding how one knows if he or she is truly in fellowship with the living God. In our postmodern world where subjectivity and relativism often seem to be our only anchors, John's dichotomy may strike us as overly simplistic. We may be asking ourselves, *What about those shadowy areas where the light and the darkness seem to mix, where the boundaries of right and wrong seem to blur?*

Those areas are important to recognize, but too often I hide behind them rather than face up to my wrongdoing responsibly and with humility. It reminds me of teaching my writing students how to assess the credibility and authority of the sources they use in their research papers. "Which do you trust more?" I ask them. "Your observations from the next table when my wife and I argue in the restaurant, or the version I give you in class the next day?" Most students agree that no matter how objective I might try to be, I'm still inclined to skew my retelling of the incident in my own favor. "It's just human nature," they say. But if they were to *overhear* the conversation between my wife and me, they would have a more balanced view.

Similarly, when we come before God and confess our shortcomings—both those words and actions that hurt others (usually called sins of commission) as well as our failures to act and speak when we could have (sins of omission)—we need to remember his standard of truth, not ours. John's words make the distinction simple because he trusts that the Holy Spirit is at work in our hearts and that his readers truly want to fellowship with God. Bottom line: Sin and fellowship with God are mutually exclusive. While my motives for any given action may be mixed, I'm usually aware at some point of what I need to confess. Can I still justify my hurtful words to my coworker or the reason for keeping the extra ten bucks in change from the cashier? You bet. But my experience has been that shortly thereafter, I become convicted of my prideful justification and have *it* to confess on top of my other faults. While I typically loathe any formula that promises success for the Christian life, I find John's equation foolproof:

Confession of Our Sins + Forgiveness in Christ = Obeying and Walking Like Jesus

When I'm tempted to justify my sins, when I'm inclined to overlook my means to an end, when I'm confused about which direction to take in the fork of temptation's road, this standard clarifies and settles the muddy waters of my emotional circumstances. There's something incredibly liberating about acknowledging that my desire to know God is stronger than my desire to protect and defend myself. Let's consider the source of such confessional power as we look at a few more questions about this passage in 1 John.

Taking It In

6. Based on these verses, how would John define "confession"? What would he consider its role to be in the Christian's journey?

7. Why did John emphasize that Jesus is the "atoning sacrifice" not only for his readers but also for "the whole world" (2:2)?

8. What do you believe John meant by the "old commandment"? the "new commandment"? (2:7-8) What is the intersection point for these two commandments?

9. What do you suppose it means that darkness blinds the eyes of one who hates (2:11)?

10. In what way does this metaphor accurately depict the consequences of hating someone? How might this motivate us to confess?

11. How would you describe John's tone in this passage? Underline
    or list below the words in the text that support your descrip-
    tion of John's awareness of his audience and his feelings about
    his subject matter.

Have you ever driven along an unfamiliar highway in the wee morning
hours without the warm glow of streetlamps to herald the way? What if
you turned off your car's headlights? Darkness would totally consume
your vision of the highway. Similarly, if we fail to confess our sins, we are
turning off the light that illuminates the path of our Christian journey.

Such disorientation in the dark often occurs during times of overwhelming stress and burnout. I'm either so consumed by busyness that I
overlook my need to confess, or I'm so desperate to maintain control of
my chaotic life that I refuse to confess, either out of fear (can I *really* trust
God with these major issues in my life?) or pride (do I *have* to trust God
with these major issues in my life?). During these seasons of duress, one
of my heaviest burdens becomes the weight of my sins, the parcel of them
held tightly by the iron fist of my self-control. My faulty thinking seems
to run something like this: Life is overwhelming me right now; if I yield
myself before God by admitting my mistakes and asking for forgiveness,
then I'm making myself vulnerable; if I make myself vulnerable, then life
will run me over.

This formula, unlike John's equation, is flawed. The great paradox of
my Christian life is that I become stronger and more resilient in battling

the hardships of life when I yield my heart to my Abba Father, my Creator who knows and loves me best. What feels like weakness—letting down our defenses before him—actually refuels our ability to rely on and trust in his goodness. Honest confession, like the self-inventory in chapter 1, requires a laying down of our defenses, a ban on the arms with which we defend ourselves most of the time. Only then can we find true rest.

Making It Real

✎ 12. Can you think of a time in your life when you deceived your-self about something you were doing or thinking? What was the context for this self-deception (feelings, circumstances, etc.)? What did it finally take for you to recognize that the truth was not in you?

13. What barriers in your life often hinder your willingness to confess? How have you dealt with these barriers in the past? Based on this passage, what would John's advice to you be?

14. Think about a time you walked in the light with God. Now think about a time you stumbled in the dark with yourself. In what ways did these experiences differ? What was the hardest part of finding your way out of the dark?

15. Spend some time reflecting on this passage in 1 John and on any areas of your life it brings to mind that need to be brought into the light. Write down some of these areas below or in a separate journal or notebook.

The power of Spirit-fueled confession opens up the clogged arteries of our heart and allows grace and mercy to circulate. Spiritual progress along the path of repentance cannot happen without a contrite spirit poured out before God. When I'm struggling and juggling too much with all that life brings, I find that a regular time of confession helps me maintain my spiritual balance. What does this look like for me? I find that I need to make sure that I have at least one weekly appointment with God to discuss my failures and shortcomings and to acknowledge my need for his grace. Also,

I try to keep communication and accountability flowing in my relationships with my wife, my children, and a few close friends. This combination of a regular period for nothing but prayerful confession along with consistent checkups with the key people in my life allows me to restore perspective on my own needs, limitations, and desires. Most of all, it keeps me moving closer to the heart of God, into the light of his goodness and the warmth of his love.

SPIRITUAL THERAPY

Imagine that you are writing a letter to a group of believers who are younger and less mature than you. You might envision your audience as your own children as adults, a group of college students, or someone you nurtured in his or her faith. Your audience has told you that they are sure of their salvation, but they are confused by the variety of denominational practices, self-help books, and motivational ministry conferences. They want to know what they need to grow in their faith and in their fellowship with God. What will you tell them in your letter? What will you tell them about the role of confession in nurturing the Christian life? (You might want to write your ideas in your journal.)

RESOURCE BIBLIOGRAPHY

Books

Crime and Punishment, Fyodor Dostoevsky, novel—A sprawling Russian epic focused on issues of justice—divine, political, and personal—as illustrated by the consequences of one man's desperate crime.

Godric, Frederick Buechner, novel—A contemporary classic that describes the trials of a twelfth-century "saint" as he seeks to reconcile his longing for God with his life in the flesh.

To Kill a Mockingbird, Harper Lee, novel—*The* Southern novel of the
twentieth century, exploring racial tensions, injustice, and
integrity through the eyes of a young girl coming of age.

Films

Crimes and Misdemeanors—Woody Allen's exploration of a successful
man's conscience as he discovers his own capacity for sin in
order to save his reputation. (This film may not be suitable for
all viewers due to graphic language and implied sexual situations.)

Dead Man Walking—A stunning film of great power and depth based
on a Catholic nun's ministry to a convicted death-row inmate
as he confronts his past crimes. (This film may not be suitable
for some viewers due to the powerful, but discreet, images of
implied violence.)

The Mission—An epic film of personal and cultural corruption and
redemption set among the eighteenth-century colonization
efforts in South America.

To Kill a Mockingbird—An Academy Award–winning adaptation of
Harper Lee's Southern classic. Gregory Peck portrays a small-
town lawyer in the South, forced to defend a black man
accused of raping a white woman during the 1930s.

Music

"Softly and Tenderly," hymn—A traditional favorite for altar calls that
reminds us of Jesus' patience and tenderness toward us when
we stumble on our journeys.

GRACE:
AN ACHING CURE

2 CORINTHIANS 12:1-10

But where sin increased, grace increased all the more,
so that, just as sin reigned in death, so also grace might
reign through righteousness to bring eternal life through
Jesus Christ our Lord.

—ROMANS 5:20-21

One of the hardest parts of watching my father battle cancer was seeing the effects of his treatment. Certainly the fatigue and weight loss caused by the growth of cancer cells in his body bore a terrible witness to the power of the disease. The chemotherapy used to treat his disease, however, appeared to take an even more drastic toll. The nausea, hair loss, and bone-weariness caused us all to wonder if the treatment was worse than the disease it was attempting to eradicate. But as severe as the side effects were, the toxic chemicals provided my family's only hope of controlling the kudzu-like growth of cancerous tumors in my dad's body.

It struck me during this time that my dad's chemotherapy had a lot in common with grace. At times it seems easier to give in to the cancer of my own sinful efforts and self-protective justifications than to humble myself before the Lord. My failures and selfish shortcomings provide the occasion for my need to confess, but that means I must acknowledge my need for God's grace every day—and sometimes this cure seems more painful than my sin.

Certainly grace is the richest of gifts, our only hope for becoming Christlike. But our reliance on grace each day means that we also must acknowledge the liability of our lifelong struggles. If we're going to experience the cure and if we want the healing God offers us, then we must face the awful reality of our dis-ease.

BREAKING GROUND

What problem have you encountered in your life that required a solution or treatment almost as painful as the problem itself? Whether it's the price tag for a new transmission or the unpleasant taste of cough syrup for our cold, most of us have experienced some level of discomfort as we have sought to eliminate some obstacle in our lives. Have you ever considered the price of accepting God's grace in your life? What is it costing you right now?

∽◦∾

Perhaps my metaphor troubles you. After all, grace is God's free gift—not something we have to pay for—as if we could afford it if we tried. True. Or perhaps you've never recognized that the very lifeblood of your Christian faith might be a bit bittersweet as well. Yet, I'm convinced that if we don't recognize the cost of living out of grace instead of our own efforts, we may be stunting our own spiritual growth. If we don't realize that our sanctification is a minute-by-minute process even though our salvation is complete in Christ, then we are likely to be disappointed and frustrated when certain habits follow us like a stray dog or old addictions gnaw at our hearts. Such frustration only compounds the weariness of soul that many of us experience amidst heart-numbing busyness.

Such is the reality of living in the tension between two worlds—this fallen world with all its unrighteousness, and heaven, full of God's glory. Even as we are saved from our sins by the gift of Christ's sacrifice on Calvary, we are not yet perfected and totally conformed to his image. We're in the process—the process of repentance, of daily turning away from ourselves and turning toward God. However much we desire to follow the narrow path toward him, we often find ourselves at cross-purposes with his grace.

It's not just my experience from which I draw this observation. Scripture provides numerous examples and exhortations instructing us to count the cost of following Christ. One passage in particular comes to mind from Paul's second letter to the church at Corinth. **Read 2 Corinthians 12:1-10** to investigate what Paul shares concerning his own experience of God's grace. Please note that because of the complex dynamics between Paul and his original audience, I suggest reading Eugene Peterson's rendering in *The Message* for its clarity. This is the translation I will quote from in the questions that follow.

FIRST LOOKS

1. Describe Paul's progression from "the matter of visions and revelations" (verse 1) to his own "humiliations" (verse 5)?

2. Based on the language in this passage, describe Paul's tone regarding his spiritually blessed acquaintance (verses 2-5)? Underline or list the words from the passage that reinforce your description.

3. What ongoing internal struggle did Paul face? What helped him overcome his pride (verses 6-7)?

4. What limitations did Paul say he had? How did he initially respond to his handicap? How did he respond to it at this point in his spiritual journey?

5. What was Paul forced to do in order to appreciate the gift of God's grace (verse 10)?

What paradox did Paul write about at the end of this passage?

During Paul's day, Corinth buzzed as the center of commerce and culture in the Greek world. Pagan religions pervaded the ancient city. Many of the members of the new Christian church in Corinth came out of this pagan background and continued to struggle with the aftershocks of immorality and idolatry that surrounded them. Paul's first letter to the Corinthians addressed many of their problems—divisive factions in the church, legalism and lawsuits, questionable behaviors, and the misuse of spiritual gifts. By the time he wrote his second letter to the Corinthians, Paul was addressing a new set of issues, mostly personal, in the fledgling church. False teachers had captivated the Corinthian Christians and turned them against Paul and his teachings. They criticized every aspect of the apostle to the Gentiles, from his appearance and speech to his alleged pride and prejudice. Paul's colleague Titus visited the church and defended his friend and comrade, and as a result, most of the Corinthians resumed confidence in the apostle. After receiving this news, Paul sent another letter to the church, reinforcing his authority in Christ and expressing thanksgiving for their repentance. Paul also addressed the still rebellious minority in the church. In 2 Corinthians 10–13 (which includes our passage above), Paul attempted to balance the uniqueness of his individual experience with the universal revelations of God's grace.

In *The Message* we see Paul's conversational tone and slightly defensive style emerge even as he transcended the situation at hand to expound the power of God's grace in everyone's weakness, not just his own. This accounts for his reluctant boasting and his self-deprecating attitude: Paul wanted to reinforce his Christ-based apostolic authority without inflating his own ego.

Since this passage is so specific in its contextual dynamics, such a personal exchange between Paul and his audience, you might wonder how we can appropriate its message in order to embrace the joyful cost of grace in our own lives. Let's reflect on some possible ways to interpret this part of Paul's letter.

Taking It In

6. Why do you think Paul brought up the experience of his "enlightened friend" but refused to describe his own visions and revelations? What effect does this have on the rest of the passage?

7. Why did Paul insist that he didn't want anyone imagining him as anything other than a "fool…on the street" (verse 6)? How

does his self-deprecation strike you—as humorous irony, false humility, careful strategy, humble sincerity, or something else? Why?

⁂ 8. Based on this passage, what do you believe Paul's handicap (traditionally translated "thorn") was—a behavior, an attitude, a physical ailment, or something else? Explain.

Why do you suppose Paul didn't specify the details of his handicap?

9. How had Paul grown into the spiritual maturity that qualified him as an apostle of Christ's truth? What's bittersweet about such growth?

10. What does it mean to "just let Christ take over" (verse 10)? What might this have looked like in Paul's life?

So much of life revolves around the ebb and flow of pain and pleasure, of trials and triumphs. Paul's keen awareness of this truth is evident in most of the letters he writes to the various churches he has nurtured in the faith. He knows the cost of discipleship, from shipwrecks and imprisonment to beatings and false accusations. And he also knows the joy of seeing the tinder of fragile believers in new churches blaze with Spirit-filled empowerment and enthusiasm.

Throughout these up and downs, Paul learns the secret to the process of repentance and spiritual refreshment. It's the simple yet impossible formula most of us have learned: less of me and more of Jesus. But living out this process can feel like enduring chemotherapy of the soul. We not only face the reality of life's trials and disappointments—the foreclosures and divorces, the layoffs and stillborn dreams, the bitter betrayals and the secret struggles—but we face them with humility and dependence on God. We don't run to our own devices, our own self-sufficiency and control. We run to the shelter of his wings and hide in the tower of his strength (see Psalm 61:3-4). Thus, when we are most tempted to make life work the way we want it to, we are most in need of yielding to God. When we feel most afraid and uncertain, we are compelled to trust him and act in faith. In my experience, such tension can be incredibly wrenching. But the implications of such words from the apostle Paul can encourage us to persevere and remind us that any temporary suffering we may experience produces for us an "eternal weight of glory."

Making It Real

11. If you were forced, like Paul, to defend your reputation as a follower of Christ, what evidence would you cite?

   What qualifies you as an example of the Christian faith to those around you?

12. Describe a time when your spiritual high or mountaintop experience came crashing down because you overlooked your weaknesses. What did you learn from this experience? In what ways has such an experience changed or deepened your faith?

13. In what ways have you seen God's grace redeem your own handicaps in life?

Name one area of weakness in your life in which you would like to experience more of God's strength? What must you do to appropriate his grace for this weakness?

14. How would your spiritual journey differ from day to day if
    you learned to "take limitations in stride"? What would it
    look like, specifically, for you to "just let Christ take over"
    (verse 10)?

This "let go and let God" truth can easily become a cliché that perpetu-
ates denial, spiritual dissonance, and secret sins. Too often we interpret
this notion as a license for passivity, as a friend of mine did when he lost
his job a year ago. He has a wife and four children to support, but he's
turned down several job offers because he's waiting on God. Now, I don't
doubt his sincerity, and I certainly cannot judge how and when our Lord
speaks to his individual children. But my friend is living in denial about
his circumstances and their impact on his family because he's afraid of taking the wrong job or switching careers.

In my own life, my frustration with painful circumstances often leads
me to give in to my weaknesses—to "self-medicate." I want to trust God
with my Ph.D. exams and overdue bills, with my children's innocence and
my father's cancer, but I get anxious and scared and sink into my weakness—the desire to feel better immediately—rather than turning to God
for the strength to tough it out. In his loving-kindness God forgives and
comforts me and challenges me to get back on my feet, to do my part, and
trust him the next day. But the accumulated toll of my refusal to turn to
God often means I feel doubly ashamed of my secret sins—for the act
itself and for my refusal to trust in God's goodness and sovereignty.

Grace means being so overwhelmed by life and its burdens, and so
disappointed in your own resources and weak willpower, that you're forced

to trust God. I can't follow my kids every second of every day, but I know One who does. I can't heal my father's cancer, but I know One who can. I can't shake all my fears and insecurities, nor has God taken them away yet, though I've asked him to much more than Paul's three times. But I can turn them over to him, acknowledging them with the honest intensity of the psalmist or the apostles. Perhaps that is the ultimate gift of his grace to us: the ability to express our fears and failures even as we face the same temptations again and again. The ability to hope in something far greater than what we can imagine, even as we stumble and struggle toward heaven.

SPIRITUAL THERAPY

What areas of your life currently occupy most of your time and attention? What specific weaknesses do you face in each of these areas? In your journal or on a piece of paper, make a chart, listing these current weaknesses across the top. Draw vertical lines down the page so that each weakness has a column. Now draw a horizontal line through the middle of the page. On the far-left side, write "me" on the top row and "God" on the other row. Okay, you probably see what's coming. Try to describe how you handle the weakness in each column, compared to how God handles your weakness.

For example, you might list "insecurity" at the top of one column, based on your current career instability at the office. You might describe your response to this insecurity as "Makes me want to eat more" or "Makes me overvalue money and material things." Then in the "God" column, you might describe how he can perfect his grace and strength through your insecurity. You might even list truths from Scripture having to do with the security you have through faith in your Abba Father. If you're feeling especially creative, you might forgo language and *draw* your descriptions, or you could clip images from magazines to create a collage.

RESOURCE BIBLIOGRAPHY

Books

Amazing Grace: A Vocabulary of Faith, Kathleen Norris, autobiographical
    lexicon—Offers personal stories and fresh definitions for sev-
    eral dozen "religious" words.

Four Quartets, T. S. Eliot, poetry—One of the most significant works of
    twentieth-century poetry, a four-part tapestry uniting personal,
    cultural, and spiritual memories.

Rich in Love, Josephine Humphries, novel—A contemporary Southern
    novel tracing the disintegration of one family's relationships
    before they are reinvented through grace and forgiveness.

What's So Amazing About Grace? Phillip Yancey, nonfiction—An inves-
    tigative, meditative report on this most unique quality of the
    Christian faith that distinguishes it from other belief systems.

Winter Garden, Pablo Neruda, poetry—A newly translated collection of
    the great South American poet's exploration of paradox and
    hope during seasons of winter.

Films

Chocolat—A movie more about how people often attempt to live outside
    of grace than about how they resist the sensual confections.

Sense and Sensibility—An Academy Award–winning adaptation of Jane
    Austen's classic social comedy of manners.

Spitfire Grill—A film that raises questions about the practical conse-
    quences of grace and personal change within a young woman's
    new community.

Music

"Adagio KV 356," Mozart—An excellent composition for reflection by
    the greatest of composers.

"Berceuse in D flat major," Chopin—A classical piece that lends itself to considerations of beauty within dissonance.

Give Me Jesus, Fernando Ortega—A contemporary Christian album of great simplicity, beauty, and lyrical grace.

Reconciled, The Call—Late 1980s rock meets the essential truths of living out of God's grace.

FORGIVENESS: DEEP BREATHING

LUKE 7:36-50

If you, O LORD, kept a record of sins,
O Lord, who could stand?
But with you there is forgiveness;
Therefore you are feared.

—PSALM 130:3-4

In recent months as I've searched for some way to include exercise in my weekly routine, I've discovered a love for swimming. Being self-taught, I've never been a particularly good swimmer, but I've always enjoyed the water, especially the cool sensation of gliding through a placid pool or a glassy lake. I like the way swimming requires my whole body to work together to reach a successful motion that will propel me through the water.

Through experience and experimentation, I've also discovered that the greatest challenge in swimming is breathing. Let me confess that I've always found it difficult to immerse my head underwater; I'd much rather keep my face above the water despite how much drag it adds. But after several weeks of such strenuous effort, I became willing to look straight down into the water and turn my head to breathe only when my burning lungs were about to burst. Try as I might, I could never go but a few strokes underwater without needing the sweet gulps of air grabbed at the surface. But this method proved equally frustrating. Then, eventually, I developed a regular rhythm that allowed me to time my breaths with my strokes so that I never ran out of air.

During one of my swimming workouts, it hit me how much forgiveness is like the air I so often take for granted. Until I'm willing to acknowledge my sins in a time of confession, I'm rarely aware of how immersed I am in myself and in my own needs and wants. The irony is, of course, that I'm also drowning. My self-absorption often feels like a soothing hot tub until I discover how far below the surface I've slipped. Without air, I get stuck in the stagnant pool of self, when I desperately long for the great ocean beyond where I can breathe freely. Breathing in the air of God's forgiveness on a regular basis allows me to move beyond my own limitations and failures, my own sins, toward his love and acceptance of me. When faced with the density of my own shortcomings, the forgiveness and grace I so often take for granted become a most precious commodity.

BREAKING GROUND

Can you swim? How did you learn to pace your breathing with your strokes in the water? How does your experience with swimming, or some other physical activity, reflect your attitude toward forgiveness? What is it about forgiveness that makes it so hard to experience on a daily basis? What is it about *us* that makes forgiveness so hard to live out and to live out of?

∽o∼

Ernest Hemingway told the story of a personal ad that appeared in a newspaper in Madrid: "Paco, meet me at the Hotel Grande at noon on Saturday. All is forgiven, Papa." Local police could not contain the mob on Saturday when eight hundred young men stormed the plaza to get into the hotel. Hemingway cited the apocryphal tale to show the popularity of the name "Paco" for Spanish men. But he inadvertently illustrated the desire all of us have to be forgiven. Whether it's the prodigal son deciding that he can no longer exist in the pig trough of his mistakes or the prostitute realizing that the love she longs for will never be found in her client's billfold, our longing to be cleansed of our failures cuts to the heart of who we are and who we are created to be. None of us enjoys carrying around the accumulation of soul debris that obscures our view and numbs our heart. We know that as long as we are saturated by our sins, we cannot absorb the sustenance of the abundant life: God's love.

We may have realized that there's a kind of reciprocal relationship between our experience of God's forgiveness and our willingness to forgive others. Never is love harder than when someone offends us. In his great philosophic dialogue *The Republic,* Plato even suggested that the worst injustice of all is to be wronged by someone without having the recourse of vengeance. Most of us have experienced such moments: the venomous words circulating about us at the office that finally reach our ears, the silent withdrawal of our spouse when we long for connection, the violation of our innocence by an abuser during our childhood, the superior look from another member of our Bible study group. Every day, in small or great ways, the sins of others carve graffiti into our hearts. Some of the painful etching fades by the next week; sometimes it penetrates so deeply that scars swell and linger for the rest of our lives. These large wounds, especially, seem impossible to overcome. What would ever compel us to forgive our boss's betrayal, our spouse's infidelity, or an abuser's violation?

We can probably relate to Plato's assumption that the desire for vengeance comes to us naturally. However, Jesus makes it abundantly clear that we are to suffer others' assaults and transcend the consequences by forgiving our assailants. And he knows, of course, how difficult—no, how impossible—this is when we rely on our own human resources. That's where the reciprocal power of forgiveness comes into play.

Jesus addressed this dilemma when his disciples asked him, "Lord, how often shall my brother sin against me and I forgive him? Up to seven times?" Jesus responded, "I do not say to you, up to seven times, but up to seventy times seven" (Matthew 18:21-22, NASB). In other words, there is no formula or clinical procedure to make forgiveness happen—it's a daily, ongoing process. Jesus follows up this insight with the parable of the wicked slave who begs forgiveness of a huge debt from his master but then refuses to extend grace on a small debt owed him by another. The master then demands exact payment from the wicked servant, since he would not show grace to his own borrower. The connection comes through loud and clear: "My heavenly Father will also do the same to you, if each of you does not forgive his brother from your heart" (Matthew 18:35, NASB).

Some believers interpret this parable as well as Jesus' statement in the Lord's Prayer—"Forgive us our debts, as we also have forgiven our debtors"—as meaning that God only forgives us in direct proportion to our forgiveness of others. This is not the reciprocal relationship that I believe exists between our experiencing God's forgiveness and our forgiveness of others. In fact, it's the inverse. If God only forgives us to the extent that we forgive others, then the entire process pivots on our ability to forgive rather than on God's supernatural willingness to forgive. No, I believe that we must first become aware of the darkness of our own interiors before we can appreciate the cleansing light God shines into us. Only then, as we taste this life-giving air of repentance, can we give mouth-to-mouth resuscitation to those around us.

Such gratitude connects us to the one Power Source who can forgive the most heinous offenses. Then we become a conduit of his grace, his mercy, and his sacrificial love to others. There may be no better picture of such gratitude and its relationship to forgiveness than the scene we find in **Luke 7:36-50.** Read this passage and then consider the following questions.

First Looks

1. Describe the scene in which this encounter takes place. What details help us envision this moment?

2. What was Simon's primary objection to the woman's presence at this party (verse 39)? What was Jesus' response to his objection (verses 40-42)?

3. According to the parable in this passage, what is the relationship between the amount of our debt and our capacity to love (verses 41-42,47)?

4. What comparison did Jesus make to reinforce his parable (verses 44-46)? What conclusion emerges from the parallel actions Jesus listed (verses 47-48)?

How startling this encounter must have been for everyone involved. Let's start with the last person to arrive. What courage it took for this sinful woman to make her way, uninvited, to the home of a man hosting dinner guests. Talk about crashing a party—this wasn't just any man's house; it was the home of a Pharisee, one of the most prominent religious leaders in the city. Not only is she not invited, but she's a woman, and one with a bad reputation to boot. Although the passage is not specific about the woman's sinful life, many scholars believe her sins were probably sexual in nature—perhaps she was promiscuous or was a prostitute or both. So before she ever uncorks the alabaster jar of perfume, a rare and expensive gift in its own right (probably containing myrrh imported from Syria or Egypt), she pays a steep price in humility just by walking through the door.

Next consider the outrage of Simon the Pharisee and the incredulity of his other guests. They are speechless as the stranger lets down her hair to dry the tear-washed feet of the Christ before she anoints them with sweet perfume. Could this really be happening—a stranger, a Jewish woman known for her immorality, in *his* house, at *this* party, doing *that?* It had to be a first. Notice Simon's response: It's not just that he's upset about having to set another place at the table; Jesus' acceptance of the woman's gift calls into question his claim to be the Messiah. Surely One so holy would never permit this kind of woman to touch him and anoint him with such sensual tenderness. Surely the true Messiah would see through this woman's audacity. What a farce!

Finally, we come to the calm, compassionate, and receptive Figure with the weeping woman at his feet. While it seems evident that Jesus is not surprised by the woman's gift nor repulsed by her reputation, he is still moved by her offering. It is startling that no words are exchanged between them—at least none are mentioned here—as she gives such a sensual and personal gift. It is not erotic in its sensuality, but all the more reason perhaps for men such as Simon to question the woman's motive as well as Jesus' motive in accepting her actions. This scene offers us a glimpse of intimacy as profound as the mystery of sexuality and as innocent as a child unwrapping a present on Christmas morning. As Jesus makes clear by his parable as well as by his comparison of the woman's actions with his host's inaction, forgiveness forges a debt of gratitude strong enough to shatter our judgment of others.

Notice, too, that Jesus does not overtly defend the woman's actions, but instead he allows Simon's own judgment of the woman to condemn him. Jesus responds with the parable of the two debtors, a simple story with a profound conclusion. When someone cancels our debts, we find that our gratitude rushes in to fill the void where our indebtedness once existed. Consequently, those who are forgiven much will love much, and those who are forgiven little will love little. This message is reinforced and applied specifically to the case at hand. As host, Simon would be expected in his culture to take care of his guests—to offer them water to rinse off the road grime from their sandaled or bare feet, to greet them with a kiss of welcome, and to refresh them with a soothing anointing of aromatic oil. These three customs would be expected of any good host. And yet Simon failed in all three; he offered Jesus none of them. On the other hand, the sinful woman is under no cultural obligation to give Jesus anything. However, she provides cleansing for his feet from the most personal source possible, the well of her tears, and dries them with a towel of her own hair. She kisses not his cheek but his feet. And she doesn't simply anoint him with a smidge of household oil, she breaks out the best, most expensive perfume she owns. The short version of this comparison might go something like this: Simon was expected to give his guest something and gave nothing. The woman was expected to give nothing and gave everything. The implications are startling and convicting for us as well. Let's work through the following questions before applying this truth to our own lives.

TAKING IT IN

5. Think about the setting of this event—a home, an everyday dinner, a woman coming in uninvited. Why is this setting so critical to our understanding of forgiveness?

   In what ways does forgiveness often require concrete action? In what ways does forgiveness often require risk taking?

6. Why do you suppose no words were exchanged between the woman and Jesus as she washed and anointed his feet? What was communicated through her actions that words could not convey?

7. Similarly, what was communicated by Simon's actions that went beyond the words he spoke? What did his actions reveal about how he regarded other people? about how he regarded Jesus?

8. How do you explain the relationship between forgiveness and love? How is this relationship demonstrated within this scene?

⚘   9. What do you suppose Jesus meant when he told the woman, "Your faith has saved you; go in peace" (verse 50)? Based on this passage, what's the relationship between forgiveness and faith?

Much of this scene's power emerges from the contrastive responses of Simon and the woman. The Pharisee seems suspicious of Jesus' identity and power, reluctant to believe that the Messiah could tolerate the presence of, let alone the very personal offering of, a sinner. The woman, however, seems oblivious to what anyone but her Savior thinks of her. She has experienced the renewal of a supernatural cleansing within. While she may have struggled to grasp the reason behind the Messiah's response to her, a sinner, she acts out of her heart without allowing her lack of understanding God's loving-kindness to impede her response to it.

Now consider whom you would rather face as your accuser and judge if you were caught red-handed committing a crime—the woman or Simon? I believe most of us would prefer to face the woman because we would be more likely to be forgiven. She knows the depths her own sinful selfishness and therefore extends the same mercy she's been shown to those around her. The implications for our own responses to forgiveness—both receiving and giving—emerge like a deep inhalation of air within our lungs. When we breathe in the life-giving forgiveness of Christ, we can then breathe out life-offering forgiveness to those around us. Let's return to the passage and consider some other more specific applications.

MAKING IT REAL

10. What does it cost you to accept God's forgiveness? How do you usually respond to his gifts of mercy and grace in your life?

11. What prevented Simon from showing the same humility and sacrifice the woman did?

In what ways are you like the sinful woman in your response to forgiveness?

In what ways are you like Simon?

12. How do you usually feel after spending some time confessing or reflecting on your sins before God? How often does your experience of confession leave you feeling humbled, indebted, and grateful? What keeps you from responding this way?

13. How would your present life differ each day if you knew, truly knew deep down in your bones, that you are forgiven? How would this awareness affect your response to those who hurt and offend you?

✐ SPIRITUAL THERAPY

If you knew that Jesus would be at a dinner party and that you would have an opportunity to give him a present to show your gratitude to him, what would you offer? After spending some time in confession, take time to create something that you would give to him. Since it's difficult to find adequate words to express the immensity of our gratitude, try to create something that doesn't require language. You might make a collage with various photographs, magazine clippings, fabrics, and craft materials to depict your understanding of forgiveness. You might want to paint a small canvas with the colors of forgiveness or compose a song expressing your gratitude.

If you're not feeling inspired to create in these ways, consider what gift of service you could give Jesus this week. Perhaps you could volunteer at a nursing home or retirement facility, at your church, at a shelter or mission. You might take your kids to the park unexpectedly and play whatever they want to play; you might plan a special meal alone with your spouse in which you take care of all the details. Your gift could even be one of showing self-control, such as refusing to retaliate when the latest office politics kills your project. You need not tell anyone why you're doing what you're doing—just let it be the unspoken essence of a sweet perfume between you and your Savior.

RESOURCE BIBLIOGRAPHY

Books

As I Lay Dying, William Faulkner, novel—A classic story about one
        family's grief and their inability to forgive one another, set in
        the great writer's mythic South.

Atticus, Ron Hansen, novel—A contemporary tale of a father's search for
        his lost son and the forgiveness needed, on both their parts, to
        bring them together.

Emma, Jane Austen, novel—A comedy of manners set in eighteenth-
        century England that portrays a young woman's journey from
        self-absorption to sacrificial love.

The Great Gatsby, F. Scott Fitzgerald, novel—This beautifully written
        portrait of the 1920s Jazz Age offers another mythic glimpse of
        the way that past mistakes resurface in present desires.

Films

Emma—A film adaptation of Jane Austen's matchmaking heroine who
        must learn her own lessons of humility and grace before she
        can love.

Magnolia—A multifaceted look at how the longing for connection and
forgiveness often has poignant and tragic repercussions. (This
film may not be suitable for some viewers: graphic language,
some sexual situations, and partial nudity.)

The Royal Tenenbaums—A darkly funny family album tracing dysfunc-
tional lifelines among an elite, intellectual—but keenly human
and petty—family in New York.

The Straight Story—A beautiful, simple story of an old man's unortho-
dox journey cross-country to find his brother and reconcile
their differences before the brother's imminent death.

Music

"A Long December," Counting Crows, on the album *Recovering the
Satellites*—In this upbeat ballad, a contemporary rock band
explores the need for reconciliation and how difficult it can be
to reach.

"Grace Greater Than Our Sin," hymn—A classic reminder of God's
ability to meet us in our need for him.

Stones in the Road, Mary Chapin Carpenter—A reflective, honest collection of folklike ballads and upbeat acoustics from a great contemporary songwriter.

GRATITUDE:
A SOUL TONIC

PSALM 107:1-9

Come, Thou Fount of every blessing,
Tune my heart to sing Thy grace.
Streams of mercy, never ceasing,
Call for songs of loudest praise.

—ROBERT ROBINSON,

"COME, THOU FOUNT OF EVERY BLESSING"

Jagged peaks jut up beyond the placid lake like teeth from a giant's jaw. I'm standing, shirtless, in the cool high-country breezes beneath a July sun. These mountains in their symmetrical, triangular formation glint with streaks of mica and burgundy sediment, with bands of icy snow clinging to their shadowed crevices. They're called the Maroon Bells, and as one of the most photographed sites in the world, they are synonymous with the splendor of the Colorado Rocky Mountains. I've taken an afternoon away from the writers' conference I'm attending in nearby Aspen to hike and bask in the awe of the Bells. It's one of my favorite and most sacred places.

On the rugged path to Crater Lake, I hear the rush of water echoing and glimpse a thaw-sprung waterfall from a peak's western slope. I stop beneath a canopy of evergreen and take a deep breath. I'm not sure why tears brim in the corners of my eyes.

But deep down, I know. It's been so hard. The grind of a full-time graduate study program, the responsibility of my full-time teaching job, the commitment to my full-time family—the full-times have overlapped to the point where there's little room for my own spirit or the Holy Spirit to operate. And it's been too long since I truly worshiped God and communicated with him. My attitude has lapsed into bitterness and fear; I've been in survival mode for too long, self-centered, stressed, and self-contained. But today it's as if my burdens and fears, my weariness and grief are melting away like last winter's snowpack in the summer sun, and I discover a relief and genuine gratitude inside that complements the setting. God is at work in me even when I'm blindsided by the burdens I carry. All the busyness and overwhelming demands have not diminished my longing to know him nor have they affected his loving presence in my life. I'm reminded of the words of Jesus in Mark's gospel: "This is what the kingdom of God is like. A man scatters seed on the ground. Night and day, whether he sleeps or gets up, the seed sprouts and grows, though he does not know how. All by itself the soil produces grain—first the stalk, then the head, then the full kernel in the head" (4:26-28). I've been asleep for a long time, and like a spiritually awakened Rip Van Winkle, I discover on this trail beneath the Maroon Bells that my faith is still growing, that God is still actively cultivating what he's planted inside my heart.

I'm incredibly relieved that my busyness and preoccupation with my burdens have not crushed my heart beyond what it can bear. Joy springs up as I cross through the pungent piñons and inhale their sweet wind-cleansed fragrance. Even the blister on my heel in my new hiking boots throbs with an awareness of being alive and of being given life by my Sustainer.

How did I lose sight of his provisions? And more important, how can

I stay in touch with his presence in my life when so many other forces try
to eclipse our relationship?

As I rinse my face in the cold melt-off streaming down the foot of the
Bells, I notice a smooth, dull red rock staring up at me. I pluck it from the
icy water as an Ebenezer of this day and this moment, a monument to God's
faithfulness, a reminder to give thanks each day, moment by moment.

BREAKING GROUND

Why do you suppose natural beauty and the outdoors often compel us to
reconsider larger issues in our lives? What is it about a walk along the
beach, a hike through the woods, or sitting down in a shady spot under
a tree that allows us to see more clearly? Think of a time in the last few
months when you were outside or were aware of natural beauty. Describe
it in your journal or share it with others if you're part of a group using this
study. It may have been as simple as noticing a robin in the branches
beyond your kitchen window. Perhaps you raked leaves, took a child to the
park, or planted annuals in a flower box; maybe you went cross-country
skiing or enjoyed a fishing trip. Consider how this moment influenced
your perspective on the other activities or preoccupations of your life.

∽◦∾

How has God been speaking into your life and calling you away lately?
I'm convinced that even amidst painful trials and seasons of anguish, God
reveals his presence and provides for the needs of our soul. Through his
gift of the Holy Spirit, our Lord makes it clear that abandonment and
deprivation of his presence are not issues, even when we feel most alone.
Responding to Judas's question about how Jesus would reveal himself to
others, the Lord replied that "the Counselor, the Holy Spirit, whom the
Father will send in my name, will teach you all things and will remind you
of everything I have said to you. Peace I leave with you; my peace I give

you. I do not give to you as the world gives. Do not let your hearts be troubled and do not be afraid" (John 14:26-27).

This comforting truth seems to evaporate, though, when I have forty essays to grade, another four to write, exams to study for, a manuscript to complete for my publisher, a transmission about to break down, bills overdue (how much are those late fees?), and a father dying of cancer. It feels like too much to handle. My guess is that you have your own list, your own set of claustrophobic circumstances closing in on you.

While we can't deny the reality of such hardships at times in our lives, we still have choices. We may feel powerless in the midst of crushing schedules and crisis-level events, but after we're aware of what we're feeling (our reaction), we can still choose how to proceed (our response). Fully aware that we're frail yet resilient people, because he lived as one of us, Jesus consistently reminds us to not be troubled or afraid, to not succumb to the storms of our lives. Too often we become so numbed to Jesus' presence that we slide into anger, cynicism, and bitterness. We lose sight of the calm center of our Father's love beneath the roiling surface; we overlook the comfort to be found beneath his sheltering wings.

You and I aren't alone in this slippage. The children of Israel consistently wavered and wandered, distracted and disengaged from the reality that God was leading them through their hardships. For instance, after having seen God deliver them from Egypt with sheer supernatural force (the plagues, the parting of the Red Sea), they still couldn't keep their focus long enough to avoid idolatry. While Moses went up the mountain to talk with God and receive the Commandments, the Israelites collected all the jewelry in the tribe and cast a golden calf (see Exodus 32). It's almost as if our hearts only have a short-term memory. Or perhaps more accurately, it's as if we *wish* our hearts only had short-term memories.

In our all-too-human efforts to escape pain, we often attempt to cut ourselves off from the history in our hearts. But if we try to deny the painful seasons, then we risk losing sight of moments such as the one I experienced near the Maroon Bells. That's why I'm convinced that one of the best ways we can stay anchored in the truth of God's Word without denying the harsh realities we may be experiencing is through gratitude. Gratitude for God's past provisions and gratitude for whatever he's doing in our present circumstances, even when we can't glimpse his design ourselves. Giving thanks and appreciating what we've been given—even when it's not what we think we want—unplugs our ears, clarifies our eyesight, and cleanses our hearts.

Obviously, it's easier to embrace this process when we're touched by the beauty of the outdoors or by the kind words of a friend. At such times it makes sense to "be joyful always; pray continually; give thanks in all circumstances" and to recognize that "this is God's will for you in Christ Jesus" (1 Thessalonians 5:16-18). But I believe that such moments don't just happen; they are cultivated. Oh, it's likely that, as children, we were naturally attuned to them, when every new day held unexpected treasure—a game of pretend with the pirates next door, the taste of chocolate in an after-school treat, the release of dandelion fluff on a spring breeze. We get older, though, and it takes more and more to impress us, to still us in our tracks, to awe us and remind us of a greater reality beyond the painful one we often experience. So we begin trying to make those supersized moments happen for ourselves. We collect our own resources and fashion our own idol, whatever it may be. This is the nutshell of my struggles with addictions; most likely, it is yours as well.

When we commit our heart's journey to knowing Jesus, we tire of our idols and long for the living water that only he provides. Through the support of the Holy Spirit inside us, we return again and again to a simplicity of faith that enables us to give thanks for all things, not just the events we like or the moments we find beautiful. We begin to trust, in practice, that, even though we may not feel like giving thanks, God is still in charge of his dynamic plan for us—a multilayered tapestry larger and more colorful than we can imagine. We return to a childlike appreciation of what we're given each day. Money to pay for our car repairs. The health of our children. The love of a spouse. The joy of friendship. A warm bed with sags in the shape of our body. The taste of crisp bacon on our tongue, and the smell of hot coffee. All the details that may seem corny or clichéd really can be catalysts for praise, for engaging with the present moment and what God is doing right here, right now even as you read the words on this page. What is he doing in you and for you right now? If we're willing to train ourselves to pay attention—to let go of fixating on the past or obsessing about the future—then these moments and details of life and beauty can become lightning rods of praise. Passing on the charge of remembering his goodness in the past and anticipating it in the future, they compel us to become conduits of praise in the present moment.

Perhaps no other book consistently points to these moments and this principle of gratitude as do the Psalms. **Read Psalm 107:1-9** and consider what it can teach us about cultivating a spirit of gratitude for the long haul.

First Looks

1. According to the psalmist, why should we give thanks to the Lord?

   With these reasons in mind, how should the "redeemed of the LORD" respond (verses 2,8)?

2. Notice how many times the psalmist used "those" and "they" in this passage. Whom did he include when he referred to "the redeemed of the LORD"?

3. Using the chart below, list each of the problems or needs the people of God faced and what the Lord provided in response.

People's Needs   *God's Provision*

4. What do all the needs of the people of Israel have in common in this passage? What do all the provisions of God have in common?

An old French proverb says, "Gratitude is the heart's memory." The Psalms seem to serve as a collection of such memories, an antidote to the short-term memory syndrome that leads us into idolatry and lost perspective. What I often find so striking—and comforting—about these poems is their emotional honesty coupled with their unflinching insight into God's character. They unite the human and the divine in a kind of earthy, sacred dialogue.

In Psalm 107 the heart's memory recalls not just the gifts provided by God, but the painful circumstances into which he gave such gifts. If we only focus on the gifts themselves, we become a bit spoiled and feel entitled and prone to view God as a kind of wishing well. We lose sight of our relationship with him. Instead, we must keep his gifts focused within the context of our needs. What are the needs of the Israelites in this passage? Notice that all of them relate to physical needs: the need for safety from enemies, the need for shelter from the desert wastelands, the need for water and food. God's gifts in this passage provide the very means of survival. To lose sight of the desperate wanderings in the desert, the parched throats and the empty bellies, is to lose sight of how significant a home becomes, how cold water tastes running down your insides, how the taste of fresh bread nourishes more than just the body.

This dual remembrance leads to the psalmist's main reason for praise, his thesis in this passage: "Give thanks to the LORD, for he is good; his love endures forever." It is as if the poet begins with his most compelling reason to give thanks and then reinforces it with specific evidence from the past. It's as if he's saying, "Just how much does God love us? Well, remember the time…"

The temptation to despair is part of life, even when we know what the Lord has done for us in the past. But knowing something cognitively is different from remembering with the heart, remembering with gratitude. When we give thanks for what the Lord has done, and more important, who he is, we embrace the tension between our present circumstances and our future hope. Such a memory of the heart allows us to wait, to cultivate patience, even when life's trials press in around us.

For all of the world-changing events between the time of the psalmist and our time, for all of the technological advancements and postmodern angst in which we live, I believe this truth remains just as vibrant and life restoring for us as it did for the children of Israel. Before we apply it directly to our lives, let's consider some of the implications of this passage.

TAKING IT IN

5. God does not need any evidence to "prove" his goodness to us. Why then do you suppose the psalmist called on the redeemed of the Lord to testify to his goodness?

6. What's the significance of where the people of the Lord came from—east, west, north, and south, from the desert waste-lands? In what ways are these people exiles?

7. Why do you think the psalmist focused on physical needs in this poem?

8. What psychological and emotional needs are implied or known by the physical needs addressed here—safety, shelter, food, and water?

9. Notice that this passage begins with the goodness of the Lord and ends with this goodness entering and satisfying the "hungry" soul. What's required for such nourishment to take place? In other words, what digestive process occurs between verse 1 and verse 9?

Unfortunately, gratitude is often touted as one of the patent fix-its of the Christian life. No matter how quickly your life may be going downhill, no matter how distressing your circumstances, if you simply count your blessings, everything changes for the better, we're told. It didn't take too many experiences like that for me to conclude that either something's wrong with me or else gratitude is not quite so simple as smiling and saying thank you. I imagine you've experienced this too.

I've decided that both of these conclusions are true. Something *is* wrong with me. I'm sometimes stressed, angry, troubled, doubtful, and numb in the midst of very scary life assaults. A simple thanksgiving list does not make the viselike circumstances or my human emotions any easier to cope with. However, choosing to give thanks and actively looking for God's presence in the midst of crushing trials *do* make a difference. The problems themselves may not disappear, but our surface distress melts when our hearts remember who God is—our good Abba Father whose love endures forever—what he's already done for us, and what we may be able to see of what he's doing for us right now. Such a response of gratitude leaves a wide path for God's intervention; our despair and presumption are undermined by the possibilities that hope in him always affords.

This is why, I believe, the psalmist focuses on physical needs in this passage. Our bodies run on cycles of need. No matter how much we eat or drink, we're going to get hungry and thirsty again. No matter how long we remain indoors, away from the elements, we can't overcome our own vulnerability to the heat of a desert sun. Our bodies consistently remind us of our neediness, no matter how much we deny it or pretend otherwise.

And it's not just our bodies that have consistent needs. Our hearts run on cycles of need as well. We know that we need God and a relationship with him and that we depend on him for our very essence and purpose, but all too often this reality seems distant and too different from our expectations for us to sustain hope in the heat of life's battles. In order to be truly grateful, we must remain truly needful.

When we acknowledge our need with humility and not with desperation, then we're more likely to review the memories of our heart. In those moments of need, I pluck the red rock from my desk and clutch it firmly, gratefully, in my hand. In those moments, we read the Psalms. Or we may confide on a heart-level with a friend or mentor. In the tension between the reality of our situations and human conditions and the reality of God's goodness and heart-historical evidence, we experience the soul tonic of gratitude. We start to notice what God has given us this day by removing the blinders of urgent self-preoccupation.

MAKING IT REAL

10. Why is it often so hard to trust in God's goodness in the midst of present trials, but so easy to see his hand in past provisions?

11. If you were called upon by the psalmist to testify as one of the redeemed of the Lord, what personal evidence would you cite? In what ways has the Lord provided for you physically in the past few months? In what ways has he nourished you spiritually?

12. According to the *New American Standard Bible,* Psalm 107:5-6 reads: "They were hungry and thirsty; their soul fainted within them. Then they cried out to the LORD in their trouble; he delivered them out of their distresses." How do you usually

respond when your soul "faints"? How do you typically respond to your soul's needs?

13. With what metaphor or detail do you most identify in this passage? Do you feel like your present needs are best described as hungry, thirsty, lost on the road, exiled in the desert, or chased by an adversary? Why?

14. In the chart below, list as many of your present needs as possible. (They may be physical, emotional, spiritual, abstract, or concrete.) Leave the second column blank for now, and return to it in the future to list how God provided for your needs.

My Needs   *God's Provisions*

SPIRITUAL THERAPY

Reminders of God's faithfulness can be remarkable touchstones for cultivating gratitude. In the first book of Samuel, for example, we find precedent for a unique kind of souvenir, an Ebenezer. After the Philistines had conquered Israel once, they pursued God's people even farther, attempting to drive them out of Canaan. But with Samuel as their spiritual leader, the Lord enabled the Israelites to overcome and push back the invading armies of Philistia (see 1 Samuel 4–7). "Then Samuel took a stone and set it up between Mizpah and Shen, and called its name Ebenezer, saying, 'Thus far the LORD has helped us' (1 Samuel 7:12, NKJV). Such a souvenir served as a tangible reminder of triumph that emerged from the bitter taste of defeat. As a monument of gratitude (Who could see the Ebenezer and not recall the victory over such a tiresome enemy?), the Ebenezer also became a conduit of hope, a reminder of a heart memory to sustain them through harder times ahead.

Similarly, we can make our own Ebenezers, and most likely, we already have some in our homes. In the next few days, look for a tangible symbol for "thus far the LORD has helped [me]." It might be an object you find, like my river rock from the Maroon Bells, or it might be a small artwork that you make or purchase. It could be a Christmas ornament, a child's drawing, a seashell, or a baseball. Avoid choosing something obvious, like a cross, unless it is uniquely personal in some way. Place your Ebenezer in a spot where you will see it each morning.

RESOURCE BIBLIOGRAPHY

Books

House of Light, Mary Oliver, poetry—A collection by the Pulitzer
      Prize–winning poet who finds inspiration in the natural world.

New and Selected Poems, Mary Oliver, poetry—Another beautiful collection, drawn from nature by one of America's finest living poets.

When Nietzsche Wept, Irvin Yalom, novel—Historical fiction presenting real people in fictional interactions that allow for a perspective of gratitude to transcend unrequited desire.

Films

Babette's Feast—An international favorite that portrays the price of discovering and appreciating the amazing gifts and provisions of each present moment.

Enchanted April—A film in which repressed and stressed British women during the turn of the century find rest and renewal in an Italian villa.

Music

"Come, Thou Fount of Every Blessing," hymn—A traditional anthem in which gratitude finds expression even in the tensions of life.

OBEDIENCE:
DIET AND EXERCISE

JAMES 1:19-27

By faith Abraham, when called to go to a place he
would later receive as his inheritance, obeyed and went,
even though he did not know where he was going.

—HEBREWS 11:8

When I teach a creative writing workshop, the hardest part of my job is motivating students to consider the discipline of writing. Even the most talented writers often believe they can work sporadically, whenever the muse strikes and inspiration floods their imaginations. Many of these writers dream of seeing their name in bold type beneath their poem on the pages of a prestigious literary journal or magazine. A few imagine themselves appearing on *Oprah*, regaling her with anecdotes about their great American novel. Now don't get me wrong, I am a very positive, encouraging teacher. But I also know that if these students are serious about pursuing their talent and calling, then I need to burst the romanticized bubble of literary success and ground them in the hard soil of daily writing practice.

Gradually, the students who are only infatuated with the image of the

writer (you know, the brooding *artiste* wearing Birkenstocks and scrib-
bling away in the local coffee shop) get winded by the pace and realize that
they're in love with being in love with writing, not with language itself.
Others decide the discipline required is just too demanding for their interest level and time constraints, like training for a triathlon for the rest of
their lives. But a handful of students accept and even embrace the fact that
writers write. Some days are easy, many days are not, but the process of
sitting down in front of a blank page or computer screen becomes less
intimidating and more natural. They realize, as I continue to discover
myself, that it's not the accomplishment of twenty pages a day, or seeing
your name in print or on a bestseller list that sustains the desire to write.
Ultimately, we write simply because we love language and the devices of
language, its sounds and rhythms, the stories and characters, the discoveries. Anne Lamott describes it wonderfully in her book *Bird by Bird:
Some Instructions on Writing and Life,* "Writing has so much to give, so
much to teach, so many surprises. That thing you had to force yourself to
do—the actual act of writing—turns out to be the best part. It's like discovering that while you thought you needed the tea ceremony for the caffeine, what you really needed was the tea ceremony. The act of writing
turns out to be its own reward."[1]

What does this have to do with obedience in our Christian journeys?
The discipline required to sustain a writer's journey with his or her craft
reflects the discipline required to sustain a believer's faith journey. So often
we want obedience to be easy, to be effortless, without cost or sacrifice. But
as we all know, we are human, and we fail to obey, consistently. So for most
of us, obedience doesn't come easily. I'm convinced much of this problem
results from our tendency to view obedience through the wrong end of the
telescope, just as my writing students often attempt to view their work
from the end result of public success. We think, "If I obey God in all these

---

1. Anne Lamott, *Bird by Bird: Some Instructions on Writing and Life* (New York: Pantheon, 1994), xxvi.

different areas of my life, then I must be okay in my relationship with him. My acts of obedience prove that I am a good Christian, someone who loves God." Rarely, however, does such motivation sustain us through the rocky times and rugged trials of day-to-day living. When I'm overwhelmed by work, by financial pressures, by the grievous losses of people I love, obedience seems alien and uncomfortable. I question God's goodness or sovereignty and justify my own desires. Or even if I choose to obey him and go through the motions, my heart is not in it. I'm obeying so I can feel good about myself, but in effect, I'm no different from the student who wants to look like a writer but doesn't risk putting anything down on paper.

So what does compel us to obey God and his commandments even in the hard times? I believe it's the discovery that the more we focus on our relationship with him, on experiencing his love and grace and presence in our lives, the more we will obey him. Like Lamott's metaphor of the tea ceremony, we discover that while we thought we needed to obey to be good Christians (the "caffeine" of our faith journeys), we really need the process of relating to God (the "tea ceremony") more.

BREAKING GROUND

What hobby, interest, or activity have you consistently pursued over the years? Do you love to swim, sew, play basketball, read mysteries, cook, paint, repair furniture? Although circumstances and life interruptions happen, what keeps you coming back to this activity? What sustains your commitment to this pursuit? What do you enjoy most about the activity? Why? Consider the ways in which your ongoing participation in this activity or hobby is similar to your relationship with God.

∽∘∾

Even when we passionately love God, ongoing obedience remains a challenge. To return to my writing metaphor, certainly no matter how much

I love to write, it's still hard work. It's time consuming, often tedious and mind numbing. But without a doubt, I will suffer whatever inconveniences come with the discipline of writing for two reasons: I'm passionate about writing, and I'm committed to it. In this regard, I suppose our relationship with God might be better illustrated by marriage. In our culture today, rarely do we marry someone and then expect to love him or her. No, we experience loving that person and then choose to commit the rest of our lives to cultivating that love. There may be times when the feelings of love fade, but we still maintain the commitment. Just because I'm arguing with my wife does not mean that I don't love her or that we should divorce. Nor is it license to have an affair.

Similarly, in our commitment to God, we must consider how to cultivate the relationship, not just go through the motions. Because of the unseen, mysterious nature of our relationship with him, we are often frustrated by our lack of control in the very concrete moments of car trouble, pink slips, and cancer. We may attempt to make obedience an idol rather than the fruit of our commitment to turn toward God. We'll do all the right actions and hope that God will reward us with fewer trials or more blessings. We'll do all the right deeds so that we can feel better about ourselves and not worry so much about what God thinks of who we are on the inside. We'll work hard and show him that we're really a good person.

We know this merit system does not hold true but is often the warped logic of our hearts, if not our heads. So how do we negotiate our internal need and passion for God with our external actions and responsibilities? How do we facilitate love-based obedience rather than a merit system? James addressed this relationship between faith and works in his letter to early believers from the twelve tribes who were scattered among the nations—the Jewish church cells outside of Palestine (James 1:1,19). **Read James 1:19-27** and consider his description of how faith and works are related and how their relationship can illuminate our understanding of obedience.

FIRST LOOKS

1. What progression of actions did James describe in verses 19-21? What connection did he make between listening and speaking with being slow to anger (verse 19)?

   Notice the way James moved on to the relationship between getting rid of moral filth and accepting the word planted in us (verse 21). What does self-control in these areas allow for?

2. According to James, what causes us to deceive ourselves into thinking we are obeying or growing in our faith (verse 22)?

   What can we do to overcome this tendency (verse 25)?

✍   3. What metaphor did James use to illustrate the contrast between those people who only hear and those who act on what they've heard? What are the implications of this comparison?

4. What litmus test for assessing our relationship with God did James describe in verse 26? What examples of "passing" the test did he give (verse 27)?

The tension between faith and works that James addresses here has existed throughout the history of humankind. After the fall of Adam and Eve, God established the Law as a means for his children to relate to him and his holiness. Those who loved and served Yahweh found themselves adhering to a rigorous system of laws and commandments. Naturally, the forest became obscured in the midst of cataloguing every tree. In other words, the followers of God became intent on creating checklists of dos and don'ts in order to maintain their obedience to the demanding and often complex details of God's Law. Maintaining this checklist quickly became more important than what it was designed for—facilitating relationship with the Creator. People became more caught up with impressing others with their faith than with nurturing their personal relationship with God. In addition, the need to fulfill the Law was ongoing, since people remained sinful in nature no matter how consistently they obeyed.

As we discover in the New Testament, Christ came to fulfill the requirements of the Law once and for all for all of us sinners. As Paul explains, "Therefore, there is now no condemnation for those who are in Christ Jesus, because through Christ Jesus the law of the Spirit of life set me free from the law of sin and death" (Romans 8:1-2). However, as Jesus experienced during his earthly lifetime, the keepers of the Jewish faith had evolved into strict legalists with little regard for the intent of the Law. They worked hard to keep the letter of the Law through their carefully constructed public appearance, but they did not relate with their Father in their hearts. Jesus repeatedly condemned their compartmentalized view of life: "Woe to you, teachers of the law and Pharisees, you hypocrites! You clean the outside of the cup and dish, but inside they are full of greed and self-indulgence. Blind Pharisee! First clean the inside of the cup and dish, and then the outside also will be clean" (Matthew 23:25-26).

Such a strong pronouncement seems fitting for such hypocrisy in these self-righteous leaders' lives. If I'm honest, many times I'm only too eager to spot people in my life who seem to live by the same Pharisaic system. However, I'm rarely as enthusiastic about examining my own motives and discovering the ways in which I try to compartmentalize the inner and outer parts of my life. I know that I often pretend to be patient or kind to others while secretly I'm resenting them for taking up my time or disrupting my agenda. Like the scribes and Pharisees, I worry more about what others, especially my Christian peers, think of me than being concerned about how I'm relating to God.

Sadly enough, I don't think I'm alone. In our Christian culture today, many believers obey out of a sense of duty, obligation, or merit. We either go through the motions of what we think God requires of us, believing that somehow he won't love us unless we do everything the right way—his way. Or we obey and hope that somehow we can "win" God's favor with our good-boy and good-girl behavior. On the extreme end of things, we see this mind-set fueling the claims of some who establish "obedience" as the key to a trouble-free life of health, wealth, and prosperity. This is simply not true. If we obey God out of detached duty ("That's what Christians are supposed to do") or a false merit system ("God will reward me if I obey"), which we can never fulfill, then we fail to fathom the relationship we have with our Abba Father. We fail to obey out of a loving commitment to him, out of the process of repentance that truly seeks to know and love him over a lifetime.

Returning to James's passage, we can see these false reasons for obedience falling away, being replaced by the freedom of allowing God's love to grow inside us. Let's consider some of the implications of this message.

TAKING IT IN

5. Describe the tone of this passage. How do you think James felt about his topic? How do you think he wanted his original audience, "the twelve tribes scattered among the nations" (James 1:1), to feel about his topic? Why do you think so?

6. List the instructions James gave his readers in this passage. Which ones seem more practical and specific? Which are more

abstract and general? Why do you suppose he included both kinds of instructions?

7. How do you interpret the metaphor of the man in the mirror? In what ways are people who hear but don't obey like those who look in a mirror but can't remember what they look like when they walk away?

8. James referred to those who both hear and obey as looking into the "perfect law that gives freedom." What do you think he meant by this?

In what ways does obedience produce freedom? What's ironic about this relationship between obedience and freedom?

9. What does it look like for believers to "get rid of all moral filth and...evil" (verse 21) and to "keep oneself from being polluted by the world" (verse 27)?

Based on James's admonition, what's a good way to get started in pursuing these goals?

In addition to James's letter, numerous passages in God's Word reinforce the fact that he desires relationship with us more than our "proper" behavior. Jesus explains, "If anyone loves me, he will obey my teaching. My Father will love him, and we will come to him and make our home with him. He who does not love me will not obey my teaching" (John 14:23-24).

Notice that Jesus sets up this point as an if-then statement: "If anyone loves me, [then] he will obey my teaching." A conjunctive language construction such as this typically places the causal, or independent, variable first: "If it's raining outside, then you should use your umbrella." Thus, using an umbrella becomes conditional to whether or not it's raining outside. The use of an umbrella is known as the dependent variable: It relies on what precedes it for its meaning and actualization. Most of us wouldn't say, "If you use your umbrella, then it will rain outside." All this is to say that Jesus' order in his statement is incredibly important. "If anyone loves me" serves as the independent, causal foundation for what comes next: "he will obey my teaching."

The psalmist approaches obedience from another perspective. He writes, "O Lord, open my lips, and my mouth will declare your praise. You do not delight in sacrifice, or I would bring it; you do not take pleasure in burnt offerings. The sacrifices of God are a broken spirit; a broken and contrite heart, O God, you will not despise" (Psalm 51:15-17). These words come to us from David, who, long before Christ's time, realized that God desires our repentant hearts and not merely our penitent behavior. This is the same very-human David who slept with Bathsheba and had her husband, Uriah, murdered when Bathsheba became pregnant after their affair. This is the same David who slung a smooth stone into a giant's forehead and conquered the Philistines. This is the same man who danced naked for joy before the Lord and is described as "a man after God's own heart." In other words, David's life was complex and messy, filled with victories and spiritual triumphs as well as rampant disobedience and its consequences. But throughout his faith journey, David maintained his love for the Lord, and his life reminds us that this is what will sustain us for the long haul, this is what will keep us getting back on our feet when we fall.

Keeping in mind these insights about obedience from Jesus and the psalmist, let's consider how to apply James's words to our own lives.

MAKING IT REAL

10. What role has anger played in your struggles to be obedient? How does anger impede your relationship with God?

Which is the greater struggle for you, being quick to listen or slow to speak? Explain.

11. It's tempting to think of this passage as instructing us to "just do it." What factors often derail your own attempts to obey God's Word? What has helped you persevere to act in obedience rather than simply hearing or knowing what you should do?

12. Recall a time when you acted in obedience and experienced a measure of freedom. How did God reveal himself to you through this experience? If you can't recall such an experience, in what ways has obedience constrained or inhibited you? What are the day-to-day effects of such containment?

We must make no mistake: Obedience requires suffering (such as staring down temptation), sacrifice (caring more for others than for ourselves), and discipline (following God's instruction even when we don't feel like it or don't understand why). However, obedience often takes care of itself if we focus on God and not on our behavior. When we are pursuing relationship with our Father, we tend to align our behavior with what he has established, with what he knows is best for us. As James points out, there is great freedom in this. We no longer have to worry about facing every situation as if for the first time, wondering what to do. Instead, we can trust that God is working in us through the Holy Spirit in ways that unite our actions with our heart.

SPIRITUAL THERAPY

Choose an area in which you struggle to be obedient. Write a journal entry or letter to God in which you describe your struggles in this area. You don't have to choose an area in which you have overtly failed or acted immorally; simply choose an area that currently seems challenging, frustrating, or laborious. You might want to consider why this area, in particular, plays into your weaknesses or causes you such strife.

Now, before God, ask yourself what compels you to be obedient in this area? Still yourself long enough in a time of reflection or prayer so that you can hear his response should he speak to your heart at this time. You may find yourself being led into a time of confession or thanksgiving, praise or petition. You may decide to share a description of your experience with a prayer partner or another group member if you're completing this study corporately. Or you may want to keep your time just between you and your Father. After a few days have passed, consider what actions God wants you to take in light of your time together.

RESOURCE BIBLIOGRAPHY

Books
The Genesee Diary, Henri Nouwen, autobiographical nonfiction—A personal exploration of calling and obedience based on this truly great Christian writer's extended stay in a Trappist monastery.

Les Miserables, Victor Hugo, novel—A sprawling epic of one man's search for personal redemption as he's pursued by a merciless law enforcer during the French Revolution.

A Plain Life, Scott Savage, autobiographical nonfiction—A compelling memoir of a "normal" suburbanite's journey into the faith and lifestyle of the Amish.

Films
Chariots of Fire—A depiction of British athletes competing against themselves and each other during the 1924 Olympics.

Do the Right Thing—A troubling look at racial tensions and the right and wrong choices of various members of a New York neighborhood one scorching summer.

Ulee's Gold—A thought-provoking film that examines morality within the complex layers of family and community. (A few scenes of violence may offend some viewers.)

Music

"Trust and Obey," hymn—A favorite that reminds us that true happiness emerges from faith in God and passionate obedience.

SUFFERING:
PHYSICAL THERAPY

1 PETER 2:13-25

He was despised and rejected by men,
A man of sorrows, and familiar with suffering.
—ISAIAH 53:3

Boxes of tissues. Ginger ale over crushed ice. Riccola lemon-mint cough drops. Drawn shades and my old shearling slippers. Sweatpants and my Broncos jersey. A classic Alfred Hitchcock movie, say, *Rear Window* or *Vertigo,* or maybe *Strangers on a Train.* These are the essentials when I am sick. During a bout with bronchitis last winter, I know I wore my wife's patience thinner than my favorite Indian-print blanket.

Humbling as it often is, I'm the first to confess that I'm not a good patient. Like many men (so I've been told), I have a tough time functioning when assaulted by a cold, the flu, or the dreaded sinus infection (which I seem to have several times a year). Part of the problem, I've decided, is that I'm an extremist: I want to be well and go about my normal routine, or I want to be sick and lie motionless in bed—like moss on a riverbank—watching everything go by. And the worst, as you probably know, is trying to go to work, trying to maneuver the kids, or trying to complete chores when your head throbs, your nose drips, and your throat feels like red sandpaper. Yet sometimes when I'm just coming down with something—that I'm-not-well-but-I'm-not-sure-what's-wrong-yet feeling—I'm forced to struggle through an in-between time.

Similarly, my spiritual ailments have forced me to suffer more of this kind of in-between state than I would like. When circumstances are going really well, or when times are really hard, I naturally draw closer to the Lord, either to give him thanks or to cling to him for support. But the Christian journey is not just a series of mountaintop highs and Death-Valley lows. It's the little blips within each day that often catch me by surprise and send me spiraling internally or leave me aching for comfort. Those little disappointments and ailments that accumulate and require an ongoing spiritual fortitude and maturity, such as when my wife understandably has to focus more on our children's needs than on mine, when a friend promises to call but fails to follow through, when I tell someone what I think he wants to hear rather than the painful truth, when the pipes burst or the furnace breaks.

While there are innumerable doorways into the process of repentance, one door looms large for all of us. We all suffer the delayed gratification of our longing for heaven amid the trials of this world. I know that I've been blessed with so much in my life, and I admit that I haven't endured much on the scale of human suffering. Certainly, my struggles pale next to the atrocities of war, the Holocaust, the ravages of cancer, Alzheimer's, or mental illness… But I am human and know something about suffering on a soul-level, just as you do. For regardless of our external circumstances, if we are fully alive, fully awake to the process of turning toward God, then we invariably suffer.

BREAKING GROUND

How would you describe yourself when suffering a cold, an injury, or some more severe physical ailment? What are the essentials you like to have around you in order to feel comforted? What's the hardest part of being sick for you? Are there any parallels between the way you handle physical illness and the way you suffer spiritual ailments?

∽◦∾

We suffer the in-betweenness of being sinful men and women who seem to return to our own selfish ways by default while simultaneously being redeemed image bearers of God who long for intimacy with the One who made us. We suffer the tensions pulled taut by our mortal existence in a fallen, fragmented world and by our immortal existence drawing us to a perfect, whole, and holy Home with our Father. The author of Ecclesiastes described such a tension this way: "I have seen the burden God has laid on men. He has made everything beautiful in its time. He has also set eternity in the hearts of men; yet they cannot fathom what God has done from beginning to end" (Ecclesiastes 3:10-11). Or consider how the apostle Paul explained, "Now we see but a poor reflection as in a mirror; then we shall see face to face. Now I know in part; then I shall know fully, even as I am fully known" (1 Corinthians 13:12).

We are mortal and face the futility of self-fulfillment in this life. We are immortal and have eternity set in our very beings by our Creator. We can't always see what God is up to or what his timetable is. As with a long delay between a delicious appetizer and a much anticipated entrée, we taste just enough of God's spiritual nourishment to keep us from starving but not enough to satisfy us for all time.

Often the view of this earthly life obscures the view of the other eternal life. After so many accumulated disappointments and thwarted expectations, we may numb ourselves to the anguish lying between both realities. When this occurs, we can also lose sight of hope. It seems too hard, too unimaginable to harbor hope when we face mundane losses and sorrows, let alone when we go through a divorce or lose a loved one in the Twin Towers. We may attempt to control or diminish our spiritual appetite, filling it with the junk food our earthly appetites crave; we may even try to detach ourselves from our relationship with God, either overtly (by rebellious, disobedient behavior) or covertly (by going through the motions of relationship while seething within).

But the longing endures. We may crush it, deny it, resent it. It may flatline on our soul's monitor for a while, but it remains, waiting to be resuscitated like a dormant bulb beneath a cold, hard winter's ground. Waiting for a glimmer of life, any sign of spring…and while God continues to bestow us with glimpses of heaven from time to time, the greatest source of our spring fever emanates from the Cross. Peter reminds us of this hope-sustaining vision in his letter to Jewish Christians facing persecution within the Roman Empire. **Read 1 Peter 2:13-25.** Let's explore the implications of Christ's example in some practical and personal ways.

First Looks

1. According to this passage, why should slaves submit themselves to their masters, regardless of the kind of treatment they receive (verses 15,19-20)?

   In what ways is this a logical argument? In what ways does it defy logic?

2. What is the example that Christ established for us to follow? How did he respond to the insults of others and to the harsh circumstances that led to his death (verses 21-24)?

3. What motivated Jesus to endure this kind of suffering (verse 24)? What were the consequences of his suffering (verses 24-25)?

4. What metaphor did Peter use in verse 25? How does it fit into the rest of his thesis about suffering?

Peter opens this passage by addressing men and women who had little hope that this life would get easier or more manageable: slaves. Bought and sold as property, many of these slaves had, nonetheless, found hope for eternal freedom through believing in Christ. Naturally, when their masters witnessed this new spiritual alliance, along with the growing power and influence of the early church, they were intimidated and feared that their slaves would revolt or run away. As a result, some masters beat and persecuted their slaves to compel them to renounce Christ and sever ties to fellow believers. While Peter is careful in this letter not to advocate such a renouncement, he seems to encourage his fellow Christians to suffer honorably. Why? Because as unfair and unjust as their plight might seem (keep in mind that slavery was a cultural institution at this time), they had a greater example of selfless suffering in Jesus. He embodies the holiness of God, the epitome of innocence because he is without sin, and yet he endured the greatest travesty of justice of all time. Betrayed by one of his own disciples, denied by another who loved him most, scourged by the brutal Roman system of justice, and charged guilty by a mob, Jesus faced the sharpest, most excruciating trial that anyone has ever experienced. Nailed to wood, pierced by a sword, left to die while carrion soldiers gambled for his garments.

Lest we think he is too far removed from our human intolerance of pain and injustice because he is the living God, we must remember that Jesus was fully human. There was nothing easy about most of his public ministry, let alone the last few weeks leading up to his crucifixion and resurrection. What compelled him to sweat drops of blood and pray last-ditch prayers in the Garden of Gethsemane? Two things: his love for his Father and his love for us, his sheep. Obedience remained an excruciating choice to suffer physical agony, personal humiliation, and public injustice. But his love fueled the grit of giving his all.

The same is required of us, even though we are not slaves or martyrs. Instead, our suffering may be more sublime, more psychological and emotional at times because of our different culture and social climate. But our need to follow Christ's example, to hope and trust in his very real ability to endure and transcend his suffering, is nonetheless our mainstay. We must remind ourselves daily, not just on the mountaintop or in the crisis, of the Source of our hope. Our hope is not based on how we're feeling, on how our circumstances are unfolding, or on how others are treating us. No, our hope is in Christ—the living God in a fleshly body like yours and mine. He endured suffering unto death so that we could be restored in our relationship to our Father. His wounds heal us, so Peter tells us. As we persevere in the faith, our wounds are healed when we sacrifice ourselves instead of brooding on our own pain. If we are to share in the example set by Christ's suffering, then I believe we must share his motivation: love of the Father and love of others. Let's consider the implications of Peter's words as we interpret this passage further.

TAKING IT IN

5. Why do you suppose Peter related the suffering of slaves under unjust masters to the suffering of Jesus, which led to the Cross? What do the two (slaves and Jesus) have in common? In what ways are they clearly different?

6. Do you agree with Peter that "it is commendable if a man bears up under the pain of unjust suffering because he is conscious of God" (verse 19)? Why or why not?

Similarly, do you agree that it's understandable to suffer the consequences of your own wrongdoing? Why or why not?

⚘ 7. Why do you think Peter included the allusion to Isaiah's prophecy, "He committed no sin, and no deceit was found in his mouth" (Isaiah 53:9)?

⚘ 8. Would there be any reason to suffer if Jesus had not died on the cross for our sins? Why or why not?

Peter knew that slaves would experience the stripes of a beating from a disgruntled master. Christ is thus someone with whom they can identify, but greater still, someone whose stripes can heal their own—and ours. When we commit to following Jesus, we kindle a hope in Someone so much greater than ourselves and our often feeble attempts at self-sufficiency. We are awakened by the Spirit dwelling in us. Yes, this hope means that we won't always (or even usually) get our own way, be comfortable, or understand what our Father is up to. We will endure the in-betweenness of being in the process of sanctification. Christ has already died for us, and our relationship with our Abba Father is restored. However, by following Christ's example, we enter into an ongoing process. We suffer like Christ, moving toward God, without reaching the fulfillment of our sanctification in this lifetime. We will not arrive at heaven on earth. We will only have glimpses, what C. S. Lewis called the "shadowlands," that stir up in us what we are destined to become and enjoy. We will be like Christ, and we will be with our Father in heaven.

When we buy into the fallacy that the Christian life serves as blissful anesthetic to the pain of a fallen, selfish world of people like ourselves, we set ourselves up for even greater disappointment. We either pretend that life is easier and better than it is, at the expense of our integrity, honesty, and emotions, or we become cynical, disillusioned, and disenfranchised people, continually on the cusp of chucking our faith altogether. I'm generalizing with these extremes, but most of us have floated or bounced between these poles enough to recognize them as landmarks. I'm convinced that our hope in Christ, especially in the example of his suffering, is our only compass for navigating life's treacherous seas. Consequently, our own struggles often compel us back to this compass more frequently than when we think we know where we're going. With this in mind, let's apply Christ's example from Peter's letter to our own course of suffering.

MAKING IT REAL

9. If we apply Peter's address to slaves metaphorically and not literally—as he likely intended—what are the masters to which you must yield? What do they require you to suffer?

10. In what ways does Christ's example sustain or encourage you in your own suffering? In what ways are you overwhelmed or intimidated by his example?

11. What is your typical response to suffering the spiritual discomfort discussed in this chapter?

   What recently has given you hope to persevere in your spiritual journey?

12. If other pilgrims were to watch how you handle adversity and the longing for heaven, what would they learn? What are some ways you can encourage others in their suffering?

In his allegorical work *The Great Divorce*, C. S. Lewis wrote that if we could see each other in the full reality of our spiritual condition, we would likely have one of two responses. Either we would witness the glorious beauty of a new creation in process of becoming like Christ, in which case we would be tempted to bow down and worship, or else we would see a distorted creature in pursuit of selfish desires self-destructing before our very eyes, in which case we would be so incredibly repulsed as to turn and run away. Lewis's point is that we are all moving one way or another, toward God or away from him, and while we may not be able to discern on the outside which direction each of us is heading, the reality is there nonetheless. With Lewis's metaphor in mind, I wonder if the way we choose to suffer our human condition is what either chisels us into the beauty of Christlikeness or batters us into a grotesque shell of self-absorption. Yes, suffering is part of this life, and we are all called to different stages and levels of intensity in suffering. However, how we suffer is up to us. We can suffer in ways that fuel our desire for heaven, for intimacy with our Father, for more of Christ in our shattered lives. Or we can suffer in ways that mire us in lopsided attempts at short-term relief.

I'm convinced that with Christ as our example, our personal dis-ease does not diminish but is replaced in the foreground of our lives by our growing love for God. We become more willing to risk, to step out in faith, to hope in what we cannot see or even imagine. This is the way we grow, get pruned, and grow some more in our Christian journey. This is how our suffering becomes the richest soil imaginable. "And not only this, but we also exult in our tribulations, knowing that tribulation brings about perseverance; and perseverance, proven character; and proven character, hope; and hope does not disappoint, because the love of God has been poured within our hearts by the Holy Spirit who was given to us" (Romans 5:3-5, NASB).

Spiritual Therapy

Visit a place nearby that commemorates the suffering of others in some way. You might choose a monument or a memorial in a local park or botanical garden. A museum of modern history in a nearby city would likely house many exhibits from past wars and conflicts. Or, you might choose a local cemetery, or perhaps a site where a tragedy occurred. The goal is not to become morbid, but to reflect upon the ways that other people have handled painful trials and endured suffering in their own lives. You might consider how you would have handled the same circumstances if you had been in their place. You might look for evidences of faith in their responses to these life events. End your visit with a brief prayer asking God what you can learn from this place and the suffering it represents.

Resource Bibliography

Books

Between the Dreaming and the Coming True, Robert Benson, a personal memoir—Chronicles one man's descent into a faith crisis and his reemergence as a stronger, more honest pilgrim.

The Diary of Anne Frank, autobiography—A poignant testimony to a young Jewish girl's courage during the Nazi occupation of her home in World War II.

Duino Elegies, Rainer Maria Rilke, poetry—An honest collection of elegiac poems celebrating the fragility of life, the necessity of grief, and the endurance of the human spirit.

The Hiding Place, Corrie Ten Boom, autobiography—One of the great classics of twentieth-century faith, a compelling personal work of maintaining hope in the midst of circumstantial despair.

Night, Elie Wiesel, autobiographical essay—A stunning exploration of inhumanity and injustice from a Holocaust survivor turned ethicist.

A Severe Mercy, Sheldon Vanauken, autobiography—A husband's memoir of his marriage and his conversion experience leading up to the loss of his wife to cancer.

A Stay Against Confusion: Essays on Faith and Fiction, Ron Hansen, essays—A collection of thoughtful essays that explores the power of story to nurture, sustain, and express our fears, desires, and hopes as believers.

Wise Blood, Flannery O'Connor, novel—Set in the South during midtwentieth century, a disturbing tale of a young man's attempt to discover authentic faith through obedience.

Yearning, M. Craig Barnes, nonfiction—An exploration of how we must learn to negotiate our longings for heaven while being grounded on this fallen earth.

Films

American Beauty—The Academy Award–winning film that exposes the hidden desires within each member of a contemporary suburban family. (This film's graphic language and sexual situations may risk highly offending some viewers, but it accurately depicts the emotional and psychological dis-eases that many believers and nonbelievers alike face.)

City of Joy—A successful American discovers the passionate joy that emerges when serving and suffering with the down-caste in India.

A Man for All Seasons—A historical film depicting the convictions of Sir Thomas More as he withstands pressure inflicted by his king, Henry VIII, during the founding of the Anglican Church.

Shadowlands—A bio-picture focused on the romance between
C. S. Lewis and Joy Davidman, along with Lewis's loss of
her to cancer.

Wings of Desire—The stunning film about angels who wish to experience the fullness of humanity, including the joy of suffering.

Music

"It Is Well with My Soul," hymn—Another traditional favorite that
reminds us of the source for true contentment amidst life's
harshest storms.

Lamenta: The Lamentations of the Prophet Jeremiah, The Tallis Scholars,
(Gimell/Polygram, 1998)—A stunning and sobering choral
suite of music based on Lamentations, ideal for reflection during challenging times.

"On Christ the Solid Rock I Stand," hymn—A classic reminder of how
to endure the most difficult times of "shifting sand."

COMMUNITY:
WOUNDED HEALERS

1 JOHN 4:7-21

*We who are strong ought to bear with the failings of
the weak and not to please ourselves. Each of us should
please his neighbor for his good, to build him up.*

—ROMANS 15:1-2

In Remy Rougeau's novel *All We Know of Heaven,* the protagonist, a young man of nineteen, enters a Benedictine monastery to fulfill his desire to live and grow in Christian community. Initially, Brother Antoine maintains high expectations for his new home and new brothers in Christ. He imagines a community united by shared peace and a blissful simplicity, where conflicts and worldly distractions have been eliminated by mutual consent to focus on the love of Christ. What he finds both disappoints and shocks him. The reality of living with several dozen other men, all at various life stages, on a working farm in rural Canada, clashes with the young novice's idealistic longings.

Antoine discovers some monks who are kind and some who are gruff and even cruel. One old monk is a pyromaniac, while another hoards useless junk and trash. Some of the men are perfectionists in their chores, while others sleep during church services. Tempers flare over the abbot's leadership to the point that one monk leaves the community. Overall, in the course of several years, Brother Antoine discovers a virtual microcosm of any human, Christian community: flawed people struggling to love one another even when they don't like each other.

Whether in the monastery or the suburbs, in our small groups from church or our committee meetings at work, we all want to connect with other people. Not only are we created as relational beings in our Maker's image (he is the Trinity), but on our Christian journeys we know that we must commit and uphold one another if any of us are going to grow in our faith. Within the common bonds of Christ, we may have experienced some of the richest friendships and most encouraging communities of our lives. On the other hand, we may have also received some of our deepest wounds and most painful betrayals. How do we overcome these scars so that we can pursue other people? How do we learn to live alongside, and even enjoy, flawed, selfish people like the monks in Antoine's monastery?

BREAKING GROUND

Who was one of your best friends growing up? What did you enjoy most about this person? What factors kept your friendship alive? Do you still keep in touch, or wish you could? Why or why not? In comparison to that early friendship, how satisfied are you presently with your connections in your community of relationships? At this stage of your life, what are the largest barriers to building relationships? What seem to be the factors that best facilitate building community in your life right now?

∽o∽

Not only are we, as image bearers of God, designed for relationship, but we are commanded to love one another by Jesus himself: "A new commandment I give to you, that you love one another, even as I have loved you, that you also love one another" (John 13:34, NASB). The problem, often enough, is the application of such a commandment. What does this look like, especially for those of us who are living out the process of repentance in our lives?

While individual relationships may vary as much as our personalities and life contexts; nevertheless, we're exhorted to think of others before ourselves; to show other people respect, kindness, and encouragement; to confront them with a bold love that points them to the Father. We know that we should forgive people when they injure us and ask for forgiveness when we hurt them. In fact, while the dynamics of our repentance (turning toward our Father) take place in us through the Holy Spirit, most of the products of such transformation display themselves in relationships. We live out our changed nature in the way we speak, think, and act toward those around us—spouses, children, parents, friends, coworkers, our church family, even strangers.

I believe that this process of *living out of our repentance* characterizes itself by three main traits: (1) a rich soil fertilized by the authenticity of the human experience—including doubt, anger, joy, fear, grief, pettiness, the whole range of emotions; (2) tools of discipline by which we challenge each other to seek God faithfully and consistently amidst the struggles of everyday life; and (3) the supernatural "rain" of Christ's empowering love. Out of this we grow and bloom. As corny as it may sound, such a garden of people remembers that we are all pilgrims in process, journeying toward what it means to know, love, and serve our Father.

As Christians, we often like to think of the local church as a place to bloom and grow; we may even limit our relationships exclusively to those within the body of Christ. Ideally, the church would flourish with these traits and facilitate our individual and corporate growth. However, as many of us have experienced, the local church can be just as disappointing as Antoine's monastery. In the church we often pretend to have our lives together on the outside even as we're drowning in sorrow, isolation, and despair. But the price of vulnerably sharing our neediness—which is perceived as weak, powerless, and less than Christian—often leads us to build even higher walls of self-protection and secrecy. It can become a vicious cycle: Disappointing relationships justify our detachment, which sets us up to disappoint others. What compels us to follow Christ's command in the midst of such downward spirals? Let's investigate another passage asserting that the foundation of how we treat each other is, indeed, Christ's love. **Read 1 John 4:7-21** and then consider the following questions.

FIRST LOOKS

1. According to John's letter, why should we love one another? What does he offer to support his argument?

2. How was the love of God made manifest among us (verses 9-10)? What effect should this have on us and on how we relate to one another (verses 11-13)?

3. Since "no one has ever seen God," what evidence of his presence in our lives can we show one another (verse 12)?

4. According to John, why is fear antithetical to love? How does perfect love drive out fear (verse 18)?

5. What does our external relationship with our brother or sister reflect about our internal relationship with God? Why did John think it's impossible to hate our brother and at the same time, claim to love God (verses 20-21)?

Since John recorded his Master's command to love in his gospel, it seems fitting that he return to this message in his letter to the early church that is struggling to assess competing claims from false teachers and divisive leaders. John returns to the foundational cornerstone of the relationship between God's love for us and our love for one another. In some respects the parallel between the two is like a trickle-down economy. The currency of God's love is so vast in its expression—the gift of his only Son to die on the cross—that when we experience its impact on our lives, we are compelled to spend our love on one another in a similar fashion.

The problem, as we have mentioned, arises when we apply this beautiful principle in a specific context with a particular group of people. Relationships, even among those who know and love Christ, can be messy. We get hurt. We hurt other people. Subtle dismissals, cynical jokes, silent rejections. Jealousy. Envy. Anger and bitterness. They pile up at times, and it doesn't seem worth the effort to work through the hard corners of our community's foundation. Yet Jesus didn't *suggest* love or offer it merely as a possibility; he commands it. Similarly, John doesn't give us any room for self-pity or isolation from others. It becomes a choice, a matter of choosing to love others even in the midst of those troublesome, painful situations and emotions.

As much as we may resent the requirements of such a command at times, it's also very comforting to know that our relationships do not depend entirely on us. If not for the supernatural love of Christ empowering us through the Holy Spirit, we would likely withdraw or distrust others permanently. Through this power source of love, we remain willing to persevere in our relationships—suffering, forgiving, confessing, exhorting each other to a deeper, more mature faith. And while it's painful, this process of relating to others reminds us all of how much our Father loves us. With this in mind, let's return to the passage from John and think through further implications of his reflections on Christ's command.

Taking It In

6. Count the number of times the word "love" appears in this passage. Why do you suppose John repeated this word so frequently, even at the risk of diluting its meaning with each repetition?

7. Considering that this is a rhetorical or persuasive passage, how did John make his case for the reasons we must love each other?

   How convincing is this "proof" when you compare it to your experiences with other people? Why?

8. What do you think John meant when he wrote, "No one has ever seen God; but if we love one another, God lives in us and his love is made complete in us" (verse 12)?

9. How does love cast out fear? What do you suppose it means to be "perfect in love" (verse 18)?

⚘ 10. Why did John make the distinctions between loving who we can see (our brother), and loving who we can't see (God)? How should this tension between seeing our brother and not seeing God affect the way we love?

Authentic community is permeated with the love of Jesus—a sense of compassion, strength, caring, and boldness that we see consistently throughout out Savior's life. In fact, his love fuels and redeems the other two traits of community that I listed earlier. Without the love of Christ, our soil of authenticity can become a fallow patch of self-absorption. Without his love, the tools of discipline can become self-righteous legalism, similar to what Jesus confronted in the Pharisees of his day. The empowering love of Christ reveals itself in our willingness to bear the burdens of others, to care when they don't seem to care, and to remind each other of who we are and who God remains. Loving with the love of Christ, as John describes in his case for its essential role in community, means living out of faith with our hearts tuned to hope.

Thanks to the example of God's gift of his Son, and the Son's gift of his atoning death and resurrection, we can love one another. Consequently, we can experience something of the divine in our earthly relationships. Since we don't see God face to face, we have to demonstrate his love to one another, becoming the hands and feet of his body. Such moments of intimacy with our Father and with one another offset the numbing despair and overwhelming isolation of our postmodern world. It's a matter of survival. For all of us.

MAKING IT REAL

11. When have you experienced the love of God through the presence, words, and/or service of another person? In what ways did this encounter affect the quality of your faith journey?

12. Consider whether there is a relationship in your life at present in which you need to demonstrate the love of God through Christ in tangible ways. Perhaps you could offer to baby-sit for a mother of young children, visit an older member of your church, or surprise a friend with a card of encouragement. Write down some ideas or talk about them in your group. Pray about who may need you to love them today.

13. What is the most challenging aspect of John's passage on love for you personally? Why?

14. What does it look like for you to love others because of what you've experienced of God's love? How is this different from what you might otherwise use as the basis for deciding when and how you love others?

15. What fears in your life hinder your ability to love others—fear of rejection, fear of intimacy, fear of vulnerability, fear of betrayal? What compels you to risk loving even in the midst of these fears?

With passionate movement toward God as our priority, we experience community that, while never perfect, can soothe our hearts with the balm of his loving presence. Despite the awkwardness, the struggles, and the betrayals, our relationships with others provide one of the richest contexts for our spiritual growth. Even though we can't see our Father physically, we see him reflected in the eyes and actions of those around us—and they see him in us.

SPIRITUAL THERAPY

As you reflect on this chapter, spend some time writing in your journal about where you are in your most important relationships with other people: family, friends, other community members in your life (such as neighbors, coworkers, members of your Bible study). To whom are you most connected? To whom could you go to confess your sins and darkest fears or your most disappointing defeats? What usually keeps you from moving closer to these people?

After you've finished journaling, choose one person from your community circle and commit to taking one risk this week to deepen this relationship. Your action need not be dramatic or overt, but it should facilitate an opportunity for a deeper connection.

RESOURCE BIBLIOGRAPHY

Books

L'Abri, Edith Schaeffer, nonfiction—A narrative account of an experimental spiritual/teaching community established in Switzerland by the author and his family.

All We Know of Heaven, Remy Rougeau, novel—The story of a young man's coming of age during his time of commitment to a community of Benedictine monks.

The Cloister Walk, Kathleen Norris, autobiographical essays—A lovely blend of personal narrative with contemporary and historical monasticism elevates this collection into a revelation of our human need for true community.

Life Together, Dietrich Bonhoeffer, nonfiction—A theological classic in its reflection on Christ's command to love one another and its exploration of the practical implications for how we grow in community.

Mariette in Ecstacy, Ron Hansen, novel—A poetic exploration of a young woman's divine experience and its effects on her small convent community.

Our Town, Thornton Wilder, drama—An incredible look into the citizens of Grover's Corners as they realize how much they often overlook in life and in one another.

The Road to Daybreak, Henri Nouwen, autobiography—Continues the personal journey of this thoughtful writer as he leaves his high-profile ministry to live in simplicity with a community of mentally challenged adults.

The Rule of St. Benedict, various translations, nonfiction—A classic and practical set of guidelines for living authentically in community with others, not just monks and nuns.

The Wounded Healer, Henri Nouwen, nonfiction—An honest and personal description of how God uses this believer's wounds to minister to others.

Films

Cookie's Fortune—Robert Altman's small-town, Southern, dark comedy of errors revolves around the mysterious death of one of its matriarchs.

Our Town, adapted from the stage play—A powerful dramatization of the timeless story involving small-town characters coming to terms with the power of the present moment.

Waiting for Guffman—An absurdist documentary-style comedy chronicling a small town's preparations for an original musical commemorating the town's founding.

Music

All That You Can't Leave Behind, U2—A contemporary rock album that
explores numerous facets of how we relate to one another, love
one another, grieve, and celebrate one another.

Oklahoma! original Broadway cast recording—A nostalgic celebration of
small-town values and the power of community; includes
many well-known show tunes.

RENT, original Broadway cast recording—This postmodern updating of
La Boheme, set in contemporary New York, follows a band of
committed friends as they explore love, sex, and death. (The
lyrics of some songs may offend some listeners due to graphic
language and sexual references.)

COMMENCEMENT:
A SPIRITUAL RETREAT

Very early in the morning, while it was still dark,
Jesus got up, left the house and went off to a solitary
place, where he prayed.

—MARK 1:35

One of God's most restorative gifts to me is a walk outdoors. Regardless of the season or even the weather, there's something soothing about a hike along a mountain trail or a stroll around the block. If your life is overcrowded like mine, you may find the starkness of bare branches against blue sky helps restore perspective, a sense of what's important as opposed to what's urgent.

During the past few years as I've juggled grad school with my job and family, I've been forced to get up extra early in order to have time for a walk. It was hard at first to get out of my warm bed while everyone else slept, to slip into sweats as quietly as possible. But once I was out the door and down the street, it seemed worth it. Cold morning air assaulted my nose as my breath clouded in the predawn darkness. A white slice of moon over my shoulders. Stars spangled across the expanse of sky. A flat line of sunlight raising a dull pulse across the horizon. Most mornings I walked around the small lake not far from our house, sometimes greeting an early jogger or dog-walker, but usually alone with God. As I sorted through the demands of the day, the appointments and deadlines, the carried-over obligations from yesterday and weeks gone by, I could feel his presence. In the cool unlit darkness. Across the half-frozen shoals of the lake. Beyond the silent ascent of the lark or loon. I learned, and continue to learn, to focus on the present moment. To take in the deep breaths of stillness and beauty washing over me. To center myself on a purpose greater than the papers I write or the classes I teach. To refocus my attention on how much he loves me despite how I've failed.

Perhaps you have your own routine, ritual, or sacred place that inspires you to inhale the loving presence of your Creator. Or perhaps you're becoming aware of your desire to implement a regular rhythm of connection with him. I'm convinced that, like the air we breathe, we need such times to cleanse and settle our souls.

GETTING AWAY

While you are encouraged to complete the previous eight chapters in the order and manner you choose, I suggest that you save this one for last. Or you may want to begin here, stepping back from the hectic demands of your everyday world in order to assess what is most important to you. Slipping out of the powerful tide of your daily schedule can be difficult but most beneficial in helping you assess what is truly most important. If you decide to take a retreat before you begin this study, allow yourself some time—if not another retreat—to reflect on where you started. Either way, be sure to plan ahead so that you can truly get away for a substantial block of time; I recommend a half-day at the very least, a long weekend if possible.

Choose a location that will minimize the number of distractions from your inward assessment. Since our home environments usually include a ringing phone, mail to be sorted, laundry to be loaded, and other people who share our dwelling, I encourage you to find a place without the usual demands on your time and attention. An inexpensive hotel in a nearby city, a bed-and-breakfast in the country, the house of a friend who's out of town (sometimes it works to swap homes with a friend), a borrowed beach cottage or mountain cabin—any of these work well. In most areas there are ecumenical retreat centers where you can stay and share lodging and meals for a small donation. Many of these encourage silence so as to afford more alone time with God with fewer distractions. Some monasteries and convents also provide spiritual retreat space for individuals. Do some research in your church library, online, or by networking with friends. Despite how frightening it may seem to be alone with God, you should try to rid yourself of as many distractions as possible—television, newspapers and magazines, cell phones, the Internet, pagers, and Palm Pilots. Plan to spend some time outdoors if the weather permits. Take along a Bible, your journal or notebook, and if you have already completed the rest of this guide, all of the "spiritual therapy" homework you've completed.

Time to Express

I suggest that you divide your retreat time into four different phases. During the first phase, communicate with God what you have been discovering through this study and/or through observations about what is going on in your life. In order for many of us to still ourselves before God and listen to him, we first have to express the many thoughts and vent the many frustrations we're currently facing. There's no right way to do this. Some of you may want to freewrite in a journal or notebook about all that is on your mind and heart. Some of you may want to pray aloud, talking with God about your concerns. Others may want to spend this first phase praying silently or finding another means of expression: drawing, singing or playing an instrument, creating a collage that reflects your present season. My only suggestion is that you express yourself as honestly and as authentically as possible before your Father.

Time to Listen

Once you've spent some time expressing yourself and your present concerns, allow some time to listen for God's voice. To facilitate this, you might read a favorite passage of Scripture, return to one of the chapters in this guide, or listen to music. You might want to take a walk or sit quietly in front of a scenic view. Again, there's no right way—What matters most is stilling yourself before the Lord and allowing him to address your heart.

Try not to rush yourself or focus on how much time has passed. Take off your watch and put it in your pocket or purse. Try not to think about anything in particular; focus on listening, really listening, to the Holy Spirit.

After some time has passed and you're ready to move on, you may want to write in your journal what God revealed to you while you were listening to him. If you didn't hear his voice the way you wanted or expected to, you might want to describe your disappointment. In either case, try to remain relaxed and allow his peace to pass over you.

Time to Assess

After a break, perhaps for a meal or snack, plan to spend the next phase of your retreat reflecting on your experiences with *Balm in Gilead*. Make a short list of the impressions, images, and realizations that emerged from your time in this study. If you are taking this retreat before embarking on the study, then consider what you would like to experience and gain from your time in it. You might consider the following questions:

1. What areas of your spiritual life need the most attention right now? Why?

What can you do to address these areas on a daily or weekly basis?

2. What do you most want to change about your life right now? What responsibilities or relationships do you need to adjust so that you can draw closer to God?

3. What has been the most satisfying or illuminating aspect of your experience with this study? How are you different as a result?

4. What has been the most disappointing or frustrating aspect of your time in this study? What do you wish you could do differently?

5. Finally, choose three spiritual goals to pursue that will help you add balance to your life by focusing more on Jesus. You might commit to praying with a friend once a week for six months, reading a spiritual classic or another selection from the "Resource Bibliography" sections at the end of each chapter, or cutting back your time at work in order to spend more time in reflection and prayer.

As you conclude your assessment, take out your calendar and select a date for your next spiritual retreat sometime within the next six months. Make the necessary preparations to ensure your commitment to that time.

Time to Celebrate
Your spiritual retreat should conclude with some free time to enjoy some activity that you may have missed in all the busyness of your current life

season. You might take a hike, find a place to go swimming, read a mystery novel, enjoy your favorite meal at a nearby restaurant, go browsing in an antiques store, or take a drive without any destination. Choose something that you usually think you're too busy to indulge in. Try to choose something that has no particular end result or accomplishment. Let this be a time of grateful acknowledgment of how God is moving in your life and of the many gifts he's giving you.

Conclude the last phase of your retreat with a simple time of worship. You may decide to join a corporate service with other people on the retreat or visit a nearby church. Or you may wish to worship alone, playing favorite music, singing a familiar hymn, and praying over your retreat time. You may want to include Communion as part of your worship time. Whether you partake by yourself (if you are comfortable with this method) or with a local body of believers, this sacrament can be a powerful reminder of your need and Christ's provision. End your worship time by asking God to continue to sustain your Christian journey and by thanking him for how far he's brought you already.

LEADER'S NOTES

SELF-REFLECTION

Question 10. Since the lame man was healed on the Sabbath, he was being obedient to Jewish law by going to the temple to make an offering. This would have been expected of him apart from his reason to celebrate—regaining the use of his legs. When Jesus saw the man and told him, "See, you have been made well. Sin no more, lest a worse thing come upon you" (John 5:14, NKJV), he acknowledged the man's concern for his spiritual condition. At this point, the once-lame man realized that he had received an even-greater gift than physical healing: forgiveness from the Messiah.

Question 11. If you are in a group, encourage members to choose a specific area or injury that they would like to see healed. To set the tone, you might be the first to share an area ("communication with my spouse") or injury ("chronic migraines") that you feel comfortable sharing with the group. Gently encourage those who give vague replies to narrow their focus to a more specific area of woundedness, even if they decide not to share it with the group. Also, be sensitive to group members who are taking a risk by sharing their vulnerabilities.

CONFESSION

Question 3. You might need to guide group members to specific contrasting pairs in these verses to jump-start their own discoveries. For example, notice in 1 John 2:2 how John stressed that Jesus died for our individual sins as well as the sins of the world. In verses 4-5, the emphasis shifts to the contrast of "liar" and "truth." In verse 7, the "new commandment" is contrasted with the "old." Verse 8 compares the "darkness passing" and the "true light...already shining."

Question 7. Depending upon your group members' familiarity with Scripture and theological terms, you might want to explain the word "propitiation" in this passage (1 John 2:2, NASB). You might also want to mention the way Jesus' death on the cross provided the ultimate sacrifice—because he was without sin—and the ultimate victory over death in his resurrection. Jesus' gift replaced the continual animal sacrifices and temple offerings that were required by Jewish law to maintain relationship with God. Making this point is important for John in this passage because his theme is "fellowship with God," an impossibility without our acceptance of Jesus' gift.

Question 12. Clearly, this is an incredibly personal question. It might help group members feel more at ease with sharing and establish an atmosphere of trust if you initiate the sharing with your own example. Try to risk more vulnerability than they might expect, but at the same time, don't share anything that's too personal or sensitive for you. Allow time for group members to sit in silence together as they reflect on their own times of self-deception. If it's appropriate, you might want to offer a brief prayer afterward and thank God for the light of his truth that helps us see ourselves and our need for him more clearly. Be sure to thank those members who share.

GRACE

Question 8. Numerous scholars and theologians have discussed what they think Paul was referring to in this passage (2 Corinthians 12:7) as well as why he didn't specify what it was. Possibilities for the former include everything from his height (Paul is thought to have been very short) to his singleness to remorse over his past persecution of believers prior to his conversion. While we can't know with certainty why Paul referred so generally to his "thorn," we can see how his ambiguity allows each of us to identify our own areas of weakness with his.

FORGIVENESS

Question 9. When Jesus told the woman, "Your faith has saved you; go in peace" (Luke 7:50), the implication was that her trust in his ability as the Messiah to forgive her brought about her forgiveness. She acted on faith and risked public humiliation by approaching Jesus at Simon's dinner; she risked being misunderstood when she offered Jesus a footwashing and anointing. Her faith was rewarded by Jesus' favor. He accepted her offering of gratitude and took away her sin.

Spiritual Therapy. You may want to organize your group and perform a "service offering" together. The group could serve a family or older church member in need or perform an anonymous act of public service such as cleaning up a vacant lot in a nearby neighborhood. Afterward, the group could meet for a social time, a meal or refreshments, and members could discuss their experience of the group's offering. On the other hand, after discussing this option with your group, you may decide to make your offering more private and personal by preparing individual offerings. If this is the case, during the next session, you might ask if anyone wants to share his or her experience with the group, but be prepared to move on quickly if everyone prefers to keep quiet.

GRATITUDE

Question 6. The various geographic references signify two things: (1) They serve as a historical reminder to the children of Israel of their forty years wandering in the desert after Egypt and prior to entering the Promised Land of Canaan; (2) They remind the people that although they come from various tribes and places in the nation of Israel, they are all united in their annual pilgrimage to Jerusalem to visit the temple and make an offering. Consequently, Psalm 107 and others like it are called the "Psalms of Ascent" because they were sung by the people as they trekked from their various homes (in various directions) toward Jerusalem. Such a journey reminded the people that they were exiled from God unless they made their annual sin offering in the temple, just as their ancestors had been exiled from home and left to wander in the desert.

OBEDIENCE

Question 3. While the implications of James's comparison are metaphoric—one sees who he is in the mirror and then "loses" his sense of identity when he goes away—the language James uses has very concrete connotations. His diction here (verse 23) describes someone who looks in a mirror, sees that her hair is mussed, or that there's egg in his beard, and goes away without making any adjustment in his or her appearance. We are the same when we look into God's Word without making any adjustment in our behavior based on what we see there.

Question 8. James emphasizes our relationship with God's Law by using a double paradox in the phrase, "the perfect law that gives freedom" (verse 25). First, by describing the Law as "perfect," James reminds us that it's from God, the only source of perfection, demonstrated concretely in the life, death, and resurrection of Jesus. God's perfection naturally reminds us of our own imperfection and our inability to fulfill his Law perfectly; in short, our need for Christ. The other paradox emerges between "law" and "freedom." We typically think of a law as restraining or coercing us— we *can't* do something (go over fifty-five miles per hour) or we *must* do something (pay income tax). In other words, laws impinge upon our personal freedoms, usually for the benefit of a larger group or community. God's Law, however, actually frees us to do what we were created for: relationship and service to our Father. Although this "perfect law" may feel like it cramps our personal freedom, it actually liberates us from distractions of self, reminding us of our true passions and priorities.

SUFFERING

Question 7. Peter alludes to Isaiah's prophecy for at least a couple of reasons (verse 22). First, the prophetic description of Jesus is accurate, reminding us of his supreme innocence and sinless nature. Second, the prophecy resonates with the children of Israel's desire for a Messiah for hundreds of years prior to Jesus' birth. God used Isaiah to speak to this hope for a Savior and the seeming impossibility of God in the flesh, a man without sin. Peter uses Isaiah to speak into our present hope in Christ, since we are sinful and deserving of the consequences of our sin apart from him.

Question 8. By reminding us of Isaiah's prophecy concerning Christ's blameless and sinless life, Peter emphasizes the ultimate severity of his suffering. It's one thing for us to suffer the consequences of our actions, but it's another level of suffering altogether to know that we did nothing to deserve it. When we suffer trials and circumstances that seem undeserved, recalling Jesus' example reminds us of two important truths: (1) While we might not "deserve" our present trial, we are nonetheless selfish, sinful creatures if left to our own devices; (2) By comparison to Christ's wrenching agony on the cross—physical torture beyond what most of us have to endure—and his blameless life, we gain a clearer perspective on our own plight. We persevere because of the strength we have in Christ: "I can do everything through him who gives me strength" (Philippians 4:13).

COMMUNITY

Question 4. John makes it clear that perfect love is relational, a response to God's having first loved us (verse 19). Fear is reactive, attempting to avoid negative circumstances and consequences. Such fear takes the focus away from the larger umbrella encompassing the reason for loving each other: God's love for us. When we're focused on his love and motivated to serve because we love him, then even when we feel afraid at times, our fear will not control us.

Question 10. You might consider the relationship between our large commitment to love God and the way we make smaller, daily choices to honor that commitment by the way we love those around us. We show our love for God when we choose to accept his gift of salvation through Jesus. Because God is not visible to us, however, our temptation is often to compartmentalize our love for him as abstract—removed from the people and opportunities for service that are right before us each day.

FOR FURTHER STUDY

If you enjoyed this Fisherman Resource, you might want to explore our full Fisherman Bible Studyguide line. The following books offer time-tested Fisherman inductive Bible studies for individuals or groups:

TOPICAL STUDIES

Angels by Vinita Hampton Wright

Becoming Women of Purpose by Ruth Haley Barton

Building Your House on the Lord: Marriage and Parenthood by Steve and Dee Brestin

Discipleship: The Growing Christian's Lifestyle by James and Martha Reapsome

Doing Justice, Showing Mercy: Christian Actions in Today's World by Vinita Hampton Wright

Encouraging Others: Biblical Models for Caring by Lin Johnson

The End Times: Discovering What the Bible Says by E. Michael Rusten

Examining the Claims of Jesus by Dee Brestin

Friendship: Portraits in God's Family Album by Steve and Dee Brestin

The Fruit of the Spirit: Growing in Christian Character by Stuart Briscoe

Great Doctrines of the Bible by Stephen Board

Great Passages of the Bible by Carol Plueddemann

Great Prayers of the Bible by Carol Plueddemann

Growing Through Life's Challenges by James and Martha Reapsome

Guidance & God's Will by Tom and Joan Stark

Heart Renewal: Finding Spiritual Refreshment by Ruth Goring

Higher Ground: Steps toward Christian Maturity by Steve and Dee Brestin

Images of Redemption: God's Unfolding Plan Through the Bible by Ruth
        Van Reken
Integrity: Character from the Inside Out by Ted Engstrom and Robert
        Larson
Lifestyle Priorities by John White
Marriage: Learning from Couples in Scripture by R. Paul and Gail Stevens
Miracles by Robbie Castleman
One Body, One Spirit: Building Relationships in the Church by Dale and
        Sandy Larsen
The Parables of Jesus by Gladys Hunt
Parenting with Purpose and Grace by Alice Fryling
Prayer: Discovering What the Bible Says by Timothy Jones and Jill
        Zook-Jones
The Prophets: God's Truth Tellers by Vinita Hampton Wright
Proverbs and Parables: God's Wisdom for Living by Dee Brestin
Satisfying Work: Christian Living from Nine to Five by R. Paul Stevens
        and Gerry Schoberg
Senior Saints: Growing Older in God's Family by James and Martha
        Reapsome
The Sermon on the Mount: The God Who Understands Me by Gladys
        Hunt
Spiritual Gifts by Karen Dockrey
Spiritual Hunger: Filling Your Deepest Longings by Jim and Carol
        Plueddemann
A Spiritual Legacy: Faith for the Next Generation by Chuck and Winnie
        Christensen
Spiritual Warfare by A. Scott Moreau
The Ten Commandments: God's Rules for Living by Stuart Briscoe
Ultimate Hope for Changing Times by Dale and Sandy Larsen
Who Is God? by David P. Seemuth

Who Is Jesus? In His Own Words by Ruth Van Reken
Who Is the Holy Spirit? by Barbara Knuckles and Ruth Van Reken
Wisdom for Today's Woman: Insights from Esther by Poppy Smith
Witnesses to All the World: God's Heart for the Nations by Jim and Carol
      Plueddemann
Women at Midlife: Embracing the Challenges by Jeanie Miley
Worship: Discovering What Scripture Says by Larry Sibley

BIBLE BOOK STUDIES

Genesis: Walking with God by Margaret Fromer and Sharrel Keyes
Exodus: God Our Deliverer by Dale and Sandy Larsen
Ruth: Relationships That Bring Life by Ruth Haley Barton
Ezra and Nehemiah: A Time to Rebuild by James Reapsome
(For Esther, see Topical Studies, *Wisdom for Today's Woman*)
Job: Trusting Through Trials by Ron Klug
Psalms: A Guide to Prayer and Praise by Ron Klug
Proverbs: Wisdom That Works by Vinita Hampton Wright
Ecclesiastes: A Time for Everything by Stephen Board
Song of Songs: A Dialogue of Intimacy by James Reapsome
Jeremiah: The Man and His Message by James Reapsome
Jonah, Habakkuk, and Malachi: Living Responsibly by Margaret Fromer
      and Sharrel Keyes
Matthew: People of the Kingdom by Larry Sibley
Mark: God in Action by Chuck and Winnie Christensen
Luke: Following Jesus by Sharrel Keyes
John: The Living Word by Whitney Kuniholm
Acts 1–12: God Moves in the Early Church by Chuck and Winnie
      Christensen
Acts 13–28, see *Paul* under Character Studies

Romans: The Christian Story by James Reapsome
1 Corinthians: Problems and Solutions in a Growing Church by Charles
    and Ann Hummel
Strengthened to Serve: 2 Corinthians by Jim and Carol Plueddemann
Galatians, Titus, and Philemon: Freedom in Christ by Whitney Kuniholm
Ephesians: Living in God's Household by Robert Baylis
Philippians: God's Guide to Joy by Ron Klug
Colossians: Focus on Christ by Luci Shaw
Letters to the Thessalonians by Margaret Fromer and Sharrel Keyes
Letters to Timothy: Discipleship in Action by Margaret Fromer and Sharrel
    Keyes
Hebrews: Foundations for Faith by Gladys Hunt
James: Faith in Action by Chuck and Winnie Christensen
1 and 2 Peter, Jude: Called for a Purpose by Steve and Dee Brestin
1, 2, 3 John: How Should a Christian Live? by Dee Brestin
Revelation: The Lamb Who Is a Lion by Gladys Hunt

BIBLE CHARACTER STUDIES

Abraham: Model of Faith by James Reapsome
David: Man after God's Own Heart by Robbie Castleman
Elijah: Obedience in a Threatening World by Robbie Castleman
Great People of the Bible by Carol Plueddemann
King David: Trusting God for a Lifetime by Robbie Castleman
Men Like Us: Ordinary Men, Extraordinary God by Paul Heidebrecht
    and Ted Scheuermann
Moses: Encountering God by Greg Asimakoupoulos
Paul: Thirteenth Apostle (Acts 13-28) by Chuck and Winnie Christensen
Women Like Us: Wisdom for Today's Issues by Ruth Haley Barton
Women Who Achieved for God by Winnie Christensen
Women Who Believed God by Winnie Christensen